Old and Curious PLAYING CARDS,

Their History and Types from
many Countries and Periods,

by

H. T. MORLEY,

B.Sc. (Arch)., F.R.Hist.S., F.S.P.
Hon. Secretary Berks Archæological Society,
Author "Monumental Brasses of Berkshire, &c.

BRACKEN BOOKS
LONDON

This edition published 1989 by Bracken Books
an imprint of Bestseller Publications Ltd.
Princess House, 50 Eastcastle Street
London W1N 7AP, England

ISBN 1 85170 330 6

Printed and bound in Italy

The sixteen colour plates
between pages 46 and 47
first appeared in "Devils Picture Books"
by Van Rensselaer
published by T. Fisher Unwin,
London, 1892

General Index.

Acknowledgments.

I wish to tender my sincere thanks and acknowledge my indebtedness to those who have helped me in the production of this book :

Mr. Sidney Lamert for the Foreword.

Miss Swadling, Messrs. C. G. C. Williams and E. W. Dormer for proof-reading.

For help with Translations : Mr. J. N. Ponchaud (French), and Mr. Kenneth Hinton (Latin), Miss A. E. York for help with Manuscript and Index, Messrs. F. M. Bunce, W. Hayes, W. A. Smallcombe, C. Boddington, F. J. Prince and P. Palmer for practical help and advice, also the Compositors, Machinists, Block Makers and Binders who have so ably carried out my wishes.

Thanks also to the Subscribers, who have by their kind promise of support stimulated and encouraged me in my work.

King of spades, cir. 1780.

A. L. Fowler, Esq., Reading.
Harold E. Gillingham, Esq., Philadelphia, U.S.A.
Rev. Canon F. J. C. Gillmor, Reading,
Messrs. Golder, Reading.
C. G. Greenfield, Esq., Reading.
Mrs. E. Guy, Reading.
Princess Ibrahim Hassan, London.
Arthur T. Heelas, Wokingham.
D. E. Herbert, Esq., Plymouth.
Messrs. Hickmott & Co., Camberley.
E. Hill, Esq., Caversham, Oxon.
Miss Hissey, Caversham, Oxon.
Stanley Hodgkin, Esq., Reading.
Wilfred Hutchinson, Aston-under-Lyne.
Junior Army & Navy Stores, Aldershot.
Miss Kellett, Reading.
T. Rowland Kent, Esq., Reading.
Austin Knight, Esq., Ealing,
Kobenhavn, Denmark. Library of the Museum of Decorative Arts.
Sidney Lamert, Esq. Late Master, Worshipful Company of Makers of Playing Cards.
L. A. Lawrence, Esq., London.
Dr. Henri Leon, London.
A. T. Loyd, Esq., Lockinge House, Berks.
W. Lovegrove, Esq., Chelmsford.
E. H. Mander, Esq., Eversley, Hants.
H. T. Marsh, Bromley, Kent.
Milwaukee Museum, Wis., U.S.A.
W. H. Moresby, Temple, London.
L. T. Morley, Esq., Reading.
H. A. D. Neville, Esq., University of Reading.
Col. Leonard Noble, Harpsden Court, Oxon.
Mrs. K. A. Oliver, Kingston Hill, Surrey.
—. Parrot, Esq., London.
Peking, China, National Library. (T. L. Yuan).
L. N. Phillips, Ashstead, Surrey.
J. N. Ponchaud, Esq., Reading.
Harry Price, Esq., Pulborough.
F. J. Prince, Esq., Reading.
Reading Museum.
Reading Free Library.

H. C. Riley, Esq., Twickenham.
H. Robinson, Esq., Preston.
Mrs. L. Rogers, Reading.
W. Rowell, Esq., Birmingham.
W. H. Short, Esq., Erleigh Grange, Reading.
B. P. Short, Esq., Bulmershe Court, Berks.
Percy C. Skelton, Esq., London.
Messrs. Slatter & Rose, Ltd., Oxford.
Messrs. W. Smith & Son, Reading. [6].
Wm. Smith, Esq., Reading.
Society of Antiquaries of Scotland, Edinburgh.
Messrs. Stevens & Brown, Ltd., London.
Messrs. G. E. Stechert & Co., London. [3].
Rev. Percy Street, Reading. [2].
L. Noel Sutton, Esq., Reading.
R. B. Stephens, Esq., Leeds.
W. M. Sturch, Esq., Wigmore Street, W.1.
Simpkin, Marshall, Ltd., London.
E. Talbot, Esq., Caversham, Oxon.
Miss Thurburn, Reading.
Leonard Wheeler, Esq., Tilehurst, Berks.
C. G. C. Williams, Esq., Reading.
Miss M. E. Williams, Exmouth.
Dr. G. C. Williamson, Guildford.
W. G. Wilsher, Esq., London.
Reg. Wishart, Esq., Belgravia, S.W.
Miss A. E. York, Reading.

LIST OF COLOUR ILLUSTRATIONS

REFERENCES

Researches into the History of Playing Cards, and the Origin of Printing. Samuel Weller Singer. 1816.

Card Essays by "Cavendish," 1879.

Facts and Speculations on the Origin and History of Playing Cards. William Andrew Chatto. 1848.

Art Journal, 1861.

List of Specimens of Playing Cards, 1844. Societe de Bibliophile Francais.

Devil's Picture Books. Mrs. J. King van Rensseler.

Prophetical, Educational and Playing Cards. Mrs. J. King van Rensseler.

Studien zur Deutchen Kunstgeschichte.

The History of Playing Cards. Rev. E. S. Taylor, B.A. 1865.

Les Cartes a Jouer et la Cartomancie. P. Boiteau D'Ambly. 1856.

Versuch den Ursprung der Spielkarten zu erforschen by J. G. I. Breitkopf. 1784.

The Court Gamester. Richard Seymour. 1720.

Academe des Jeus. Paris, 1659.

Recherches sur les Cartes a Jouer. Bullet. 1757.

Dissertations on the History of Playing Cards. "Archæologia," 1787.

Catalogue of Playing and other Cards in the British Museum. Dr. W. Hughes Willshire. 1876..

The Symbolism of the Tarot.

Gentlemen's Magazine. 1843.

The Costumes of Coat Cards. J. A. Repton. 1843.

Special thanks to M. Rene D'Allemagne, the author of *Les Cartes a Jouer,* for kind permission to reproduce some examples from his book, published in 1906.

Subscribers.

F. Adlam, Esq., Reading.
H. Rene D'Allemagne, Esq., Paris.
W. Archer, Esq., Reading.
Miss A. R. Baily, Binfield.
—. Baker, Esq., Wantage.
W. Austin Balsom, Esq., Reading.
G. G. Barley, Esq., London.
B. T. Batsford, Ltd., London.
Miss Constance Baxendale, Newbury.
Col. Beach, Reading.
Harold Beaumont, Esq., London.
J. H. Benyon, Esq., Englefield Park, Berks.
Berks Archæological Society.
H. Blatch, Esq., Reading.
C. Boddington, Esq.; Sonning Common, Berks.
D. Boorman, Esq., Ventnor, I.W.
Milton A. Bridges, Esq., New York, U.S.A.
Warwick Cardwell, Esq., Caversham.
A. Waldegrave Carter, Esq., Caversham.
T. H. Chambers, Esq., St. Albans.
N. H. Chambers, Esq., St. Albans.
Miss N. T. F. de Chaumont, Crowthorne.
Cheltenham Public Library.
— Combridge, Esq., Hove.
Edward Cox, Esq., Mattingley, Hants.
T. T. Cumming, Esq., Reading.
—. Delagno, Esq., London.
F. G. Dennis, Esq., Reading.
T. Edw. Donne, London.
A. C. Drew, Reading.
Mrs. Drury-Lavin, Sonning, Berks.
Miss Fraser Duff, Mapledurham, Oxon.
F. G. Fedden, Esq., Cleeve, Oxon.
Dr. W. E. St. L. Finney, Kingston Hill.
A. A. Ford, Reading.

Arms of
The Worshipful Company of Makers
of
Playing Cards.

Fig I. German, page 87.

Fig. 2. Indian,
page, 55.

Fig. 3. English, page 163.

Fig. 4. German,
page 75.

Introduction.

"*To Think is to act.*"—EMERSON.

This little quotation from Emerson perhaps sums up the reason of this effort of mine to try and say something about the wonderful history and interest connected with playing cards. The quotation may also be reversed and made to say "To act is to think," for during many years spent in collecting some 200 varieties of these pieces of cardboard, ivory, lacquer, bone, cloth, &c., which have been used for playing cards, I began to think, and then (partly in response to the many enquiries for information which I received) to act, and about five years ago commenced to write a small treatise of probably 25 to 30 pages, with illustrations of a few of the cards. Once started, however, there immediately arose the difficulty of knowing where to stop. The difficulty increased as time went on, and I acquired many fresh examples for my collection, until my original plan had to be altered, and what was—in the first place—intended to be a small pamphlet has grown into a somewhat bulky volume, extending to some 240 pages with more than 330 illustrations. Yet it seems only to have touched the fringe of the subject and what has had (owing to lack of space) to be left unsaid is of infinitely greater volume than what I have been able to compress into this book.

My greatest difficulty, however (realising that there must be a limit) has been that I could only illustrate a few cards from each pack (in most cases only one or two) when, especially in the political and educational packs, every picture on each card is a part of a story illustrating a sequence of events. This particularly applies to the English cards, as in the 17th and 18th centuries every event of importance seems to have been made an apology for reproducing a sort of miniature illustrated history upon a pack of cards. Generally, one must own, these illustrations have been of a satirical character.

Whilst probably there are to-day very few subjects which are open to the charge of being comparatively unknown, works on the history of playing cards have been somewhat neglected in England. Their scarcity is particularly noticeable when one considers the many volumes which have been written upon the subject in France and Germany. The works of Samuel Weller Singer (1816), W. A. Chatto (1848), and Rev. F. S. Taylor (1865), are all out of print, and I hope, therefore, that the readers of my book will not be too hard upon my humble endeavours to bring some light upon this somewhat neglected subject.

Although I have to a large extent relied upon examples in my own collection it would not be fair to the title of my book to ignore the many other "old and curious" cards found in other collections and described and illustrated in various works which have been published and to which I am indebted for much information.

Among the splendid collections from which I have borrowed examples are those found at the British Museum and the Bodleian Library, Oxford, and also that of the Worshipful Company of Makers of Playing Cards which is housed in the Guildhall, London. In addition, there are a few private collections, and these all go to show the enormous scope and wonderful variety of the subject.

I do not claim that the few pages at the commencement are in any way a concise history. They are simply intended as an introduction, and all through I have tried to remain faithful to the idea of the title of my book and endeavoured to show and explain as many as possible of what may be really called "Old and Curious Playing Cards."

LEICESTER HOUSE,

READING, 1931.

Henry T. Morley

Atout No. VIII. cir. 1393.

Page 37.

FOREWORD

by SIDNEY LAMERT, Esq., past Master of
The Worshipful Company of Makers of Playing Cards.

It is a curious fact that, while books on all subjects which interest mankind—and a great number which do not—continue to multiply indefinitely, Playing Cards have, for half a century or more, been overlooked by authors. Of course, books about Card *Games* have never ceased to flow from the press, but these come into a different category. In the early part of the 18th century much laborious work was done in a number of European countries in delving into the origins and history of Playing Cards and the compilation of a bibliography would include many names such as Brietkopf, Singer, Chatto, Marsden, Bernoulli, Rudiger, Grellmann, D'Allemagne, &c. About 1865, the Reverend Edward Taylor published "The History of Playing Cards," in which he reviewed the work of his predecessors, while adding a certain amount of information which he had culled by his own researches; and this book, somewhat discursive and rambling, was perhaps the last serious and comprehensive work in English on the subject. In point of fact it may be doubted if there is really much more that can be added to the sum of our knowledge relating to the origin of Playing Cards. That they came from the East is established, and much ingenuity has been expended in elaborating the theory that Playing Cards were a development of the earlier game of Chess, as played with living pieces. Certainly they came to Europe in the 14th and 15th centuries, and by the middle of the 16th century were much patronised by the great nobles, and possibly by lesser folk, of that day.

In the present volume "Old and Curious Playing Cards," Mr. Morley has resolutely avoided the temptation to write learnedly or historically and has stuck to the purpose which his title indicates, namely, to give his readers a panoramic view of numbers of interesting packs produced in many countries of the world during many centuries. Mr. Morley has the flair of your true antiquary, and is at the same time a connoisseur with a broad and humorous view of life. It is not the dry-as-dust historical fact with which he has to do, so much as the very human tendencies of man portrayed in the makings of the packs of cards which he has chosen to illustrate his subject. Mr. Morley has been a collector for many years and he has supplemented his own treasures with packs culled from other sources. The result is a compilation which, while appealing more directly to those of the community who play cards, will nevertheless be of vivid interest to everyone who savours life as it has been lived during the ages by his fellow creatures.

April, 1931. SIDNEY LAMERT.

Ace of Cups, cir. 1470.

OLD AND CURIOUS
PLAYING CARDS.

MOST of the writers who have endeavoured to trace the origin of Playing Cards, agree that in all probability they came from the East, and that the Crusaders or the Gipsy Tribes (who began to arrive in Europe about the same time) introduced them into Southern and Eastern Europe, and whilst there are no historical records existing connected with games played with cards, which can go back further than the end of the 14th Century, it is thought that they were in use for games and for fortune telling as early as 1360.

The earliest cards which were known in Europe were called Tarots, Tarocchi, etc., and seem to differ somewhat from those used later, although the cards which we can trace as manufactured in the 15th Century, were no doubt derived from them. The first European packs consisted of four suits of fourteen numerical cards, one to ten, with four Coat or Court Cards = fifty-six, and besides these were twenty-two other Cards called Atouts = seventy-eight in all. The marks of these four suits of the Tarot Pack are usually Cups, Swords, Money, and Batons or Sticks, and they are no doubt the origin of our modern packs as we find these four emblems still in use in Italy, Spain, and Portugal.

The earliest undoubted mention of cards in England is 1463, in the reign of Edward IV, when by an Act of Parliament passed in that year, the importation of playing cards was expressly prohibited in consequence of the manufacturers of London and other parts of England making complaint against foreign manufactured wares which greatly obstructed their own employment. This express mention of playing cards shows that there must have been a fairly large trade in their manufacture, and that their use was well known long before.

An American writer would however take us back much further, right into the time of the Pharoahs, she says that the cards should be studied not as a game, but as the leaves of a book, and that the cards known as Atouts (which are still used in parts of Italy) are connected with Mercury (the herald of the gods) and that the symbols on the cards themselves reveal their original connection with the worship of Mercury, Thoth, and Nebo, the three gods, who were worshipped for many generations in Etruria, in Egypt and in Babylon, and she further writes:—

> "Although the gap between the old cards and the worship of Mercury of Etruria is still to be bridged through accurate historical data, the inferential connection is too strong to be ignored, and the rules of the games played with the cards intended for prophesying or fortune telling, as well as the tradition connected with the Tarots themselves, offer connecting links with the cult of Mercury that cannot afford to be disregarded, as has been done hitherto."†

Another writer, Count de Gebelin, also speaking of the old Italian Tarocchi or Tarot cards, says, that vestiges of the learning of the ancient Egyptians can be traced in the symbolic characters of the Atout cards, and his theory suggests a general history of science and art, which, as is well known, had its beginnings in ancient Egypt. When the twenty-two Atout cards are studied, not as a game of chance, but as a scientific story, we cannot help seeing the connection with many of the pictures and the mythology of the ancient world. Writing in 1781* Count de Gebelin says:—

> "That originally the twenty-two figures of the Atouts or emblem part of the Tarots were painted on the walls of the temples, a fashion inherited from Biblical times, to enable the worshippers to recognise the sciences, arts or conditions represented by the figures and their attributes when it was wished to consult them."

† Prophetical, Educational and Playing Cards, page 22, by Mrs. J. King Van Rensselaer.

* Le Monde Primitif, Vol. VIII, page 265.

To consult the gods, rods were thrown, and as they fell they would point to the various figures on the wall. These rods or arrows were marked with four different tokens, dividing them up into the four divisions or suits, which is now the number universally adopted. In the twenty-two Atout cards, when combined with the sixteen Court cards and the forty numerical cards of the Tarots can be traced (with a little imagination) illustrations of the game of life. One can read the representation of a youth with his parents or guardians, as on each card we have something expressive of human life, such as love, marriage, ambition, temperance, friendship, luck, hatred, despair, hope, success, death and resurrection, the whole presided over by the god Mercury, the writer on the tablet of fate. These Tarot packs (of seventy-eight cards) have been called *"The Bible of the Gipsies," "The Athora of the Egyptians," "The Thoro of the Hebrews," "The Great Book of Thoth Hermes,"* and *"The Key of things hidden from the beginning."***

It may be that the reason for almost invariably having four suits, is because of the four emblems that are peculiar to Mercury, *viz:*— his Cup or Chalice, his Money, his Caduceus and his Sword, that are easily recognized as representing the four classes into which the people of most nations can be divided, namely:—

The Cup or Chalice	representing	The Churchman.
The Sword	,,	The Soldier.
The Money	,,	The Merchant.
The Caduceus or Wand	,,	The Workers.

and these four emblems, Cups, Swords, Money and Sticks or Wands, are still used on the old Italian playing cards, probably just as they were when first introduced into Europe.

This investigation as to the origin of playing cards, going back to the time of the Pharoahs, (interesting as it may appear) is not within the scope of this book, and coming back to a more modern suggestion we find that writers generally agree that cards are probably an adaption of the game of chess, which originated in India or China about A.D. 450, and in which we find the King, the Horseman, the Camel and the Footmen. There was no Queen, as the Orientals would not allow a woman to be in any way part of their recreations. When introduced into Europe we find that the Vizier of the East became the Queen of the West, the Horseman became the French Chevalier and the English Knight, and Ruck the Camel became the Bishop, and so on.

** Prophetical, Educational and Playing Cards, page 173.

Breitkopf, a German writer says:—

"As the military groundwork of the game of cards, and its similarity to chess, cannot be denied; so a closer examination of this affinity may readily lead to the origin of the change in their figures and colours."

The game of Chess* is said to have been invented by Palamedes, 680 B.C., but most writers place it in the 5th Century, A.D. and it is generally agreed that it originated in India.

Because there was no Queen in the Eastern pack, it perhaps explains why in the oldest European playing cards that have been found there was no Queen, and in old Spanish packs, and in the modern ones as still found in parts of Spain and Portugal, the Court cards are King, Chevalier and Valet only, and in many German packs we still find the King, the Ober or Chief Officer, and the Unter or Subaltern, but no Queen. The Italians, however, added a Queen to the King, Chevalier, and Valet, so we get in the old Italian packs, sixteen Court cards, making with the forty numerical cards a pack of fifty-six, called the Tarots and added to these are the twenty-two Atouts, making seventy-eight in all.

In England we always think of a pack of cards as fifty-two, and the suits as Clubs, Diamonds, Hearts and Spades, and while generally speaking, most of the European countries use similar cards, we still find many other varieties not only in the suit signs, but also in the number of cards making up the pack, as well as in shape and size.

In Italy, Spain and Portugal the Suit signs are Cups, Money, Swords and Batons or Wands. In Germany, Bells, Acorns, Hearts and Leaves, and the number of cards in each pack vary very much from twenty-four, thirty-two, forty, forty-eight to fifty-six.

In the cards used in the East the number in each pack and also the shape are different from the European cards. Indian and Persian are usually circular and the packs sometimes consist of eight suits of twelve each=ninety-six, and sometimes ten suits of twelve each=one hundred and twenty. The Chinese packs (which they claim to have invented as early as A.D. 1120) have thirty or thirty-two cards which are long and narrow (about 4 inches long by ½ to 1 inch wide). The Japanese packs have forty-eight cards with flowers and signs and one plain white. They measure only 2 by 1¼.

* Caxton printed "The Game and Playe of Chesse in 1474."

Although the foregoing notes relating to the invention and history of playing cards suggest that they originally came from the East it is only fair to say there is a diversity of opinion among the various writers on this subject, many contending that the playing card that is used to-day in Europe is an original invention and not an importation.

While we have to own that there is very little, if any, trustworthy evidence relating to playing cards and their introduction into Europe previous to the 14th century, there are some curious and interesting analogies as to their connection with the East which are worth considering.

First of all, the four signs, viz:—Cups, Swords, Rings and Wands, which we find on the earliest known Tarot packs of Italy and Spain, are the same four emblems as those which the Indian Deity ARDHANARI is holding in its four hands (see Fig. 311). This certainly seems to be more than a coincidence and if these four emblems are compared with the four suit signs shown on the Spanish and Italian cards (Figs. 73, 78) the resemblance will be seen at once. It is a remarkable fact that not one or two, but all four emblems are the same, and it seems to point out very plainly that the idea of our playing cards was an importation or, at any rate an adaptation, and not an European invention.

Secondly, cards and chess have so much in common, and there is no doubt as to chess being of Eastern, probably Hindostanee origin.

In the third place, cards of the East have no Queen, and playing cards, when first introduced into Europe, had no Queen.

Then too, many Indian cards, as well as the games played with them, have a certain likeness to European cards and games. The Hindostanee cards are generally ninety-six in number, and there are three players. In the old European game of Ombre the players are only three.

Lastly, certain games played in India have much in common with European games. This is particularly the case with the game of cards known as *Ghendifeh,* where the marks of the suits and many of the rules of the game have distinct relations to the *Minchiate* which is played in Italy, and the game of *Ombre* as played in Spain. The two signs, money and swords on the European tarot cards are very similar to the same signs on the cards of India.

Although various dates, earlier than the 14th century, have been given, at which cards are said to have been mentioned, upon investigation these have generally been found not to refer to playing cards. The earliest date which has never been disputed is the one discovered by Pere Menestrier in registers of the *Chambres des Comtes* of the crazy French king, Charles VI, where the royal Treasurer, Charles Poupart, in his accounts which commence in February 1392, has made the following entry—

> "*Donne a Jacquermin Gringonneur, peintre, pour trois jeux de cartes a or, et a diverses couleurs, ornes de plusieurs devises, pour porter devers le Signeur Roi, pour son ebatement LVI sols Parisis.*"

> "*Paid to Jacquermin Gringonneur, painter, for three packs of cards in gold and colours of various devices, to present to the said Lord the King, for his diversion 56 sols Parisis.*"

This account relating to these cards has often been quoted as the origin of playing cards in Europe, but it should be noticed that the payment was for *painting* these packs for the use of the King, and not for inventing them. The bare mention of payment for doing this without any comment as to the novelty of the idea, plainly shows that playing cards were already well known. It would seem that this was a special order, and that the artist was given a free hand to produce a much more elaborate set than usual, with gold and colours, as they were for the "*diversion of our Lord the King.*"

On page 115, particulars are given of seventeen cards which are preserved in Paris and are said to be part of the three packs referred to, although some writers declare they are really part of a Venetian Tarot pack of the 15th century.

This popular idea that cards were invented as an amusement for the crazy King Charles VI of France (who lost his reason in 1392 through sun-stroke) is quite disproved by the records which relate to the Tarot and Atout packs, and to the various records where cards are mentioned. In 1240 the 38th Canon of the Council of Worcester forbids clergymen to join in disreputable games, or to play at dice, neither shall they allow games of Kings and Queens to be played, and it is thought that this reference to Kings and Queens refers to cards. But this is very doubtful as the very earliest cards had no Queen.

Many injunctions have been made at various times prohibiting clergymen to play at "dice, cardes or table playing," and even to-day in the apprenticeship forms we still find the apprentice binds himself not to frequent taverns, play cards, etc.

As man is stated to be the only animal that is capable of gambling, and as he has so often abused this power, and as cards are supposed to be the greatest evil in connection with the gambling spirit, card playing and gaming have at various times and by various people in authority been condemned or forbidden. Even the Romans issued edicts against gaming.

Many notable people have been fond of card playing and Chatto tells us that Queen Elizabeth and Queen Mary were cardplayers, but that Queen Elizabeth was a bad loser. Martin Luther played backgammon for an hour or two after dinner, in order, by unbending his mind, to promote digestion.

James I was a cardplayer, and his favourite game was Maw which appears to have been the fashionable game in his reign, as Primero was in the reign of Queen Elizabeth. James appears to have played at cards in the same way in which he played with affairs of state, in an indolent manner, requiring someone to hold the cards for him, if not to prompt him what to play.

The Vicar of Broad Hembury (Augustus M. Toplady) amused himself by playing with a few select friends one or two rounds of twopenny Pope Joan, etc. Tate Wilkinson† writing in 1790 says:—"Mr. John Wesley speaking in a field at Leeds, gave an account of himself by informing us, that when he was at College he was particularly fond of the devil's pops (or cards) and said that every Saturday he was one of a constant party at Whist, but the latter part of his time there, he became acquainted with the Lord; he used to hold communication with Him, he recollected he said, the last Saturday he ever played at cards, the rubber at Whist was longer than he expected, and pulling out his watch, when to his shame, he found it was some minutes past eight, which was beyond the time he had appointed to meet the Lord. He thought the devil had certainly tempted him to stay beyond his hour; he therefore suddenly gave the cards to a gentleman near him to finish the game, and went to the place appointed, and resolved never to play with the devil's pops again. That resolution he had never broken."‡

† "Memoirs of Tate Wilkinson," Vol. III, pages 9-11.

‡ Card playing is prohibited on all Wesleyan Church premises, according to the constitution as arranged by John Wesley.

In a sermon preached in the reign of Charles I, and published in 1627 by Samuel Ward of Ipswich, entitled "Woe to Drunkards," there is a woodcut (see fig. 5) in which the vices of that age are contrasted with the virtues of a former one. In the upper part we see the open Bible, the foot in the stirrup, and the hand grasping the lance, while in the lower part the degeneracy of the present is shown by the leg and foot decorated with a large silk bow and rosette, by a pack of cards and dice, a smoking pipe and a hand holding a glass with a cockatrice in it.*

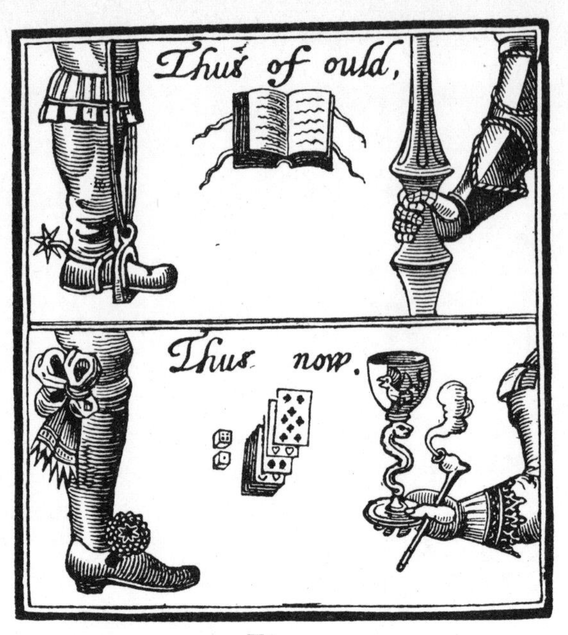

Fig. 5.

Jeremy Taylor writes:—"Many fierce declarations from ancient sanctity have been altered against cards and dice, by reason of the craft used, and the consequent evils, as invented by the Devil."

In France in 1397 (and also in the same year in Germany) a statute was passed prohibiting the use of cards except on stated occasions, and in 1404 the Synod of Langres prohibited priests and curates from playing at dice, and at cards.

In England in the reigns of Henry IV and Henry VIII in order to compel every one of the King's subjects between 7 years of age and 60, to practice shooting with the long bow—"no person was allowed for hiere and living to have any common house, etc.—or place of bowling, —dicing, tables or carding, or to haunt places so kept—and none husbandman, apprentyce, laborer or serving man, shall play at tables, tennis, dyce or cardes—out of Christmas, and then also, anywhere save in his master's house and presence."

To the Puritans, cards were the Devil's Picture Book and many pamphlets were published and sermons preached condemning their use. Lavater says:—"It is possible that a wise and good man may be prevailed on to game; but it is impossible that a professed gamester should be a wise man."

*Chatto, page 131.

John Northbrooke, a writer in the 16th century, gives a singular and curious opinion as to the invention of cards, as follows :—

> " The Playe of Cards is an invention of the Devill, which he found out, that he might the easilier bring in ydolatrie amongst men. For the Kings and Coate Cards that we use nowe, were in olde time the images of idols and false gods : which since thay thet would seeme christians, have chaunged into Charlemaigne, Launcelot, Hector and such like names, because they would not seeme to imitate their idolatrie therein, and yet maintaine the play itself."

A treatise wherein Dicing, Dauncing, Vaine Playes, and Enterludes with other idle Pastimes, commonly used on the Sabbath day, are reproved by the Authorite of the word of God and Auntient Writers, made Dialogue-wise by John Northbrooke.

The title of a pamphlet referring to the Civil War is :—

> " The Bloody Game at Cards as it was played betwixt the King of Hearts and the rest of his Suite, against the residue of the Packe of Cards wherein Is discovered where faire play was plaid and where was fowle. Shuffled in London, Cut at Westminster, Dealt at Yorke, and Plaid in the Open fiel by the City-clubs, the country spade-men, Rich Diamond men, and Loyall Hearted Men "—The rest of the pack have therefore done very well and wisely to crave a truce of the King of Hearts who is more willing to forgive them than they have bin apt to oppose him.
>
> " Since they on both sides have been cross't
> And both have wonne and both have lost.
> It now is thought high time of Day
> Friendly to part and leave off play."

There is an interesting invective against cards published in 1550 called "Il Traditor," The Traitor, which may be translated thus :—

What is the meaning of the female Pope,
The Chariot and the Traitor,
The Wheel, the Fool, the Star, the Sun,
The Moon, and Strength, and Death,
And Hell, and all the rest
Of these strange cards ?*

* Prophetical Playing Cards, page 319.

From an Old Print.

An interesting print by an anonymous engraver, marked with the date 1500, represents the Duke and Duchess of Bavaria, engaged at cards. It is remarkable that in this instance the royal pair are represented as having kept a chalked score, which seems to show that the lady is well ahead of the Duke. The only card displayed presents us with the suit of hearts, which is common to both the German and French cards.* The print demonstrates the fact that cards were a common amusement with persons of distinction in the fifteenth century.

Duke and Duchess of Bavaria playing at cards.

* Singer, page 274.

TAROCCHI & ATOUTS.

Fig. 6.

Tarocchi de Mantegna, cir. 1470.

The four cards (Fig. 6) are from a series of fifty early Italian engravings known by the various names of the *Ginoco di Tarocchi di Mantegna, Carte di Baldini, Italian Tarocchi Cards, Ancient Venetian Tarots, etc.** They date from about 1470 and are printed from engraved copper plates. They are considered by some writers to be the source from which European playing cards originated, and this relationship seems probable as we find about one-half of the Atouts of the old Italian packs have been borrowed from these ancient figures. These 50 cards are divided into 5 groups, each group containing 10 cards. It has also been suggested that about the end of the fifteenth century someone selected twenty-two of these emblematic figures and added to them a series of numeral cards which eventually became the pack of 78 as first used in Italy, made up of 22 Atouts, 16 Coat Cards and 40 numerals.

The four cards shown are No. 46 Jupiter, see Fig 6, No. 19 Clio (The Muse of History), No. 48 Octava Sphera (the 8th Sphere) and No. 49 Primo Mobile (The Chief Agent). They are much larger than the ordinary playing card, being 7 in. by 4 in.

* See Italian Exhibition Cards, page 66.

These fifty full-length emblematic figures with their symbols, are, as stated, divided into five groups of ten each, but a sequence runs through them from 1 to 50, the numbers being marked in Arabic numerals and also in Roman figures after the title, which is engraved at the bottom of each card.

The figures represented in the series E illustrate on 1 to 10 the various conditions of life, from the beggar or slave to the Emperor and Pope. Those of 11 to 20, series D, portray the Muses. Series C, 21 to 30 the Sciences, while series B, 31 to 40 give us the Virtues, and the last group A 41 to 50 symbolises the Planets or the Creation of the world.

	E		D.		C
1.	Misero.	11.	Caliope.	21.	Grammatica.
2.	Fameio.	12.	Urania.	22.	Loica.
3.	Artixan.	13.	Terpsicore.	23.	Rhetorica.
4.	Merchadante.	14.	Erato.	24.	Geometria.
5.	Zintilomo.	15.	Polimnia.	†25.	Aritmetrica.
6.	Chavalier.	16.	Talia.	26.	Musicha.
7.	Doxe.	17.	Melpomene.	27.	Poesia.
8.	Re.	18.	Euterpe.	28.	Philosofia.
9.	Imperator.	*19.	Clio.	29.	Astrologia.
10.	Papa.	20.	Apollo.	30.	Theologia.

	B.		A.
31.	Iliaco.	†41.	Luna.
32.	Chronico.	†42.	Mercurio.
33.	Cosmico.	43.	Venus.
34.	Temperancia.	44.	Sol.
35.	Prudencia.	45.	Marte.
36.	Forteza.	*46.	Jupiter.
37.	Justicia.	47.	Saturno.
38.	Charita.	*48.	Octavo Spera.
39.	Speranza.	*49.	Primo Mobile.
†40.	Fede.	50.	Prima Causa.

No. 25 Arithmetic.

Fig. 7.

1 The beggar.	11 Calliope.	21 Grammar.	31 Astronomy.	41 Moon.
2 The knave.	12 Uranis.	22 Logic.	32 Chronology.	42 Mercury.
3 The artisan.	13 Terpsichore.	23 Rhetoric.	33 Cosmology.	43 Venus.
4 The merchant.	14 Erato	24 Geometry.	34 Temperance.	44 Sun.
5 The Nobleman.	15 Polyhymnia.	25 Arithmetic.	35 Prudence.	45 Mars.
6 The Knight.	16 Thalia.	26 Music.	36 Strength.	46 Jupiter.
7 The Doge.	17 Melpomene.	27 Poetry	37 Justice.	47 Saturn.
8 The King.	18 Euterpe.	28 Philosophy	38 Charity.	48 8th sphere.
9 The Emperor	19 Clio.	29 Astrology.	39 Hope.	49 Chief agent.
10 The Pope	20 Apollo	30 Theology.	40 Faith	50 First cause.

* Fig. 6. † Fig. 7, 8, 9, and 10.

If each series is examined it will be seen that the most important subject has the highest number—50, and the least or most subordinate the first number—1. Thus, the Pope, the highest dignitary has the number 10, whilst the beggar has the lowest number, 1. Apollo, the son of Jupiter and Chief of the Muses has the number 20, whilst Urania, the daughter of Jupiter and Caliope are numbers 11 and 12 of the Series D. The most important branch of knowledge, Theologia, number 30, occupies the highest number in the Science Series, while Faith is highest among the Virtues in Series B. Finally, in the series A, the Prima Causa, number 50 is shown as the most important of all.

In Figs. 7, 8, 9 and 10 we have four of these fifty cards, No. 25, ARITHMETIC, No. 40, FAITH, No. 41, THE MOON, and No. 42, MERCURY, each with their various attributes and emblems.

Fig. 8. Fig. 9. Fig. 10.

The Twenty-two Atouts.

Count de Gebelin, writing in 1781, on "*Du Jeu des Tarots,*" says that these 78 Venetian Tarots, *i.e.*, the 22 Atouts Cards and the 56 Numeral Cards, have an unquestionable claim to be regarded as an Egyptian book which escaped the flames when the ancient libraries were destroyed, and if the Tarot game be closely investigated, it must be evident that it is based on the sacred Egyptian number, seven. Each suit or colour is composed of twice seven cards. The Atouts are in number three times seven = 21. The total number of cards being seventy-seven = eleven times seven, and the "Mat" or "Fool" being "O."

The names on the 22 Atout Cards are :—

	English.	*Italian.*	*French .*
I.	THE MAGICIAN.	IL BAGATELL.	LE BATELEUR.
II	THE HIGH PRIESTESS OR POPE JOAN.	LA PAPESSA.	LA PAPESSE.
III	THE EMPRESS.	L'IMPERATRICE.	L'IMPERATRICE.
IV	THE EMPEROR.	L'IMPERATORE.	L'IMPEREUR.
V	THE HIEROPHANT, OR POPE.	IL PAPA.	LE PAPE.
VI	THE LOVERS.	GLI AMORTI.	LES AMOREUX.
VII	THE CHARIOT.	IL CARRO.	LE CHARIOT.
VIII	JUSTICE.	LA GIUSTIZIA.	LA JUSTICE.
IX	THE HERMIT.	L'EREMITA.	L'EREMITE.
X	WHEEL OF FORTUNE	RUOTA DELLA FORTUNA.	LA ROUE DE FORTUNE.
XI	FORTITUDE OR STRENGTH.	LA FORZA.	LA FORCE.
XII	THE HANGED MAN.	L'APPESO.	LE PENDU.
XIII	DEATH.	LA MORTE.	LA MORT.
XIV	TEMPERANCE.	LA TEMPERANZA.	LA TEMPERANCE.
XV	THE DEVIL.	IL DIAVOLO.	LE DIABLE.
XVI	THE TOWER OR THUNDERBOLT.	LA TORRE.	LA FOUDRE.
XVII	THE STAR.	LA STELLE.	L'ETOILE.
XVIII	THE MOON.	LA LUNA.	LA LUNE.
XIX	THE SUN.	IL SOLE.	LE SOLEIL.
XX	THE LAST JUDGEMENT	IL GIUDIZIO.	LE JUGEMENT.

XXI	The World.	Il Mondo.	Le Monde.
	The Fool.	Il Matto.	Le Fou.

The above order is the one generally adopted, although it sometimes varies, but this is unimportant, and in giving details of these twenty-two emblematic figures, I have endeavoured to show illustrations taken from packs of different dates.

Fig. 11. 16th Century.

No. I. The Magician.

Represented by a young man standing behind a table, upon which are various articles and tools. He is sometimes called "The Cobbler," as one of the tools resembles a cobbler's awl. He is wearing a hat of mystic meaning shaped like the sign of "eternal life". In his hand is a wand, sometimes said to represent the rod of Aaron, and sometimes the caduceus of Mercury, and on the table the devices which mark the suits as used in Italy are sometimes shown, viz., Money, Cup, Sword, and Baton. See Fig. 11.

Symbol of Eternal Life.

He may also represent a Conjuror at his table as in many illustrations he holds a ball as if about to make it vanish, implying that life is but a dream—an illusion—a game of chance—and that we are under the guidance of an over-ruling administration, over which we have no control.

Fig. 12. 19th Century.

Fig. 13. 19th Century.

No. II. The High Priestess.

Shows a seated female figure between two pillars which represent the two pillars of Solomon's Temple (Boaz and Jakin). She is wearing a double crown with two horns and is holding a book, (sometimes a roll) in her hand inscribed with the word *Tora,* signifying the Secret Law. On her breast is a large solar cross and a crescent is at her feet. "The Italian card-makers," says de Gebelin, "named numbers II and V of the Atouts, Mother and Father, or Papessa and Papa," but their emblems are Egyptian, and the crown worn by number II si the one borne by Isis in the Fete des Pampylies, where Isis joyfully receives Osiris (*See No.* 10). It is the symbol of regeneration of plants, or Spring. One would not have thought it possible for this figure to be shown on an Italian pack, as it embodies the belief in a female pope, but it seems to be invariably introduced in the list of the Tarot cards, and the story probably took its rise in Germany. She is said by some writers to be the wife of the Chief Priest (No. v), and as the Egyptian priests were known to be married, it would seem to prove that these emblematical cards are by no means a modern invention, for there would be no female priest or priestess in a modern pack. See Fig. 12.

No. III. The Empress.

Shows the figure of a woman seated and holding a sceptre, with a shield, sometimes having the sign of Venus' looking-glass upon it, while in other packs an eagle is shown. (*See Fig.* 13). Upon her head is a jewelled crown with twelve stars at the points. A field of corn is at her feet, and beyond is a fall of water. She is sometimes said to represent Ishtar of the Babylonians.

No. IV. The Emperor.

Shows a figure crowned (sometimes in profile) seated on a throne and holding in his right hand a sceptre in the form of the *Crux Ansata,* the emblem of power, and is said to represent Jupiter. See Fig. 14, Fig. 16, also Fig, 170, which is shown in colours.

No. V. The Pope.

Shows a figure in ecclesiastical vestments wearing the triple crown, seated between the two pillars of the temple, his right hand uplifted with the two fingers raised in benediction, and holding in his left hand a triple-headed cross. Two or more figures are kneeling at his feet, and on some cards two large keys are shown. The Sceptre with the triple Cross* is certainly an Egyptian relic, having relation to the triple Phallus, which represents the recovery of Osiris. See Fig. 15.

* The triple cross is used as a mark of hierarchical distinction, the Pope alone being entitled to use it.

In accordance with the mystical and oriental theory of the import of the tarots, the Pope is seen extending the fingers of the right hand in benediction, or the hierophant is making the sign which prescribes silence, and which may be observed on the figure of *Ardhanari,* the Isis of the Hindus† a pantheistic emblem typifying Nature, Truth and Religion. In this Hindu emblematic figure (which has been worshipped for many centuries in India) the four symbols of the ancient Tarots are seen in her four hands, *viz.*, the Cup, the circle of Money, the Sword and the Wand or Club, and it is remarkable that these four signs should be the same as used on the playing cards first known in Spain and Italy.‡

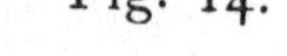
Fig. 14.

Fig. 15.
18th Century.

† Ardhanari Fig. 310.

‡ See Spanish and Italian Cards.

No. VI. The Lovers.

This card shows a young man between two females, representing vice and virtue. Sometimes the two figures are shown as a nude man and woman. Hovering overhead in a cloud Cupid with a drawn bow, is seen shooting his arrows at the young man, who stands undecided, and it would seem to indicate that he is starting out on his life's journey and his future depends upon his choice between good and evil. In fortune-telling this card denotes love, friendship, and marriage, and also luck and good fortune. See Fig. 17.

Fig. 16.

Fig. 17.
15th Century.

In an old 15th Century Pack, Atout No. IV., The Emperor, marked as V., is shown as Jupiter, with his thunderbolts in each hand and riding upon a cloud. The drawings are poor and coloured with stencils. Fig. 16.

No. VII. The Chariot.

The number seven has always been regarded as a mystic number, and plays an important part in occult science, and on this card we see a figure of a king, or conqueror, in armour, standing, in a triumphal car—generally shown as drawn by two lions—sometimes by two horses

Fig. 18. 15th Century.

Fig. 19.
18th Century.

or two oxen, and on one pack by a black lion and a white lion, both having the head of a sphinx. He holds a spear in his right hand, and a crown is upon his head. It suggests victory and triumph and in conjunction with the sevens of the pip cards, is regarded as having a peculiar occult meaning. Fig. 18.

No. VIII. Justice.

A female figure seated on a throne with a crown upon her head, holding a sword in her right hand, and a pair of scales in her left hand. She is said to represent the goddess of Justice "Astræa,"* the daughter of Jupiter and Themis, and stands for justice, conscientiousness, power and law. See Fig. 19. See also Fig. 10.

Fig 20. 19th Century.

Fig. 21. 18th Century.

No. VIIII. The Hermit.

A mysterious figure, bent with age, with a staff, and holding aloft a lighted lantern. The staff suggests a pilgrim, and this card is supposed to represent prudence, strength of character, circumspection, and love. Figs. 20 and 21.

* Astræa lived among men, but because of their wickedness, she withdrew to heaven, and was placed among the stars, under the name of Virgo.

No. X. Wheel of Fortune.

In mythology this emblem, which is one of the oldest in the world, represents Osiris, the great Egyptian divinity, the husband of Isis, judging the souls of the dead, and we see Anubis and Typhon striving to overpower each other. Anubis was an Egyptian divinity worshipped in the form of a human being with a dog's head, and was said to be the conductor of spirits to the judgement. Typhon, a monster of the primitive world, is described as a destructive hurricane. He was the brother of Osiris and is said to have murdered him and cut his body into pieces and thrown them into the Nile. This number of the Atout cards shows them working against each other at the Wheel of Fortune. Sometimes the emblems of the four evangelists are shown on this card. This emblem is also said to have its analogy in the wheels of Ezekiel* and Pythagoras. It is a satire on Fortune, (where human beings in the form of animals rise and fall,) and shows how she elevates rapidly into notice and lets fall with equal rapidity. See Fig. 22.

Fig. 22. 15th Century.

No. XI. Fortitude.

A female figure is seen forcing open the mouth of a lion expressing courage, fear, vitality and innocence. This may have some connection with the story of Una and the Lion. The figure is wearing the hat of mystery, shaped like the sign of eternal life, as Figs. 23 & 24.

* Page 47.

No. XII. The Hanged Man.

A man suspended by one foot from a gibbet with his hands tied behind his back and the other leg crossing the one by which he is suspended. The card expresses charity, courage, knowledge and prudence, as well as wisdom, and fidelity. Vulcan (the Roman God of fire) is supposed to be the god represented by the hanged man, not only on account of the strong arm, but also because he was thrown out of heaven and lamed for life. In a pack illustrated by Count de Gebelin he is shown with his feet in the same position and fastened by one foot, but instead of hanging head downwards he is standing upright and it is said that the man represents prudence, but being figured with one foot cautiously advanced before the other, which had been expressed in a Latin title as "*pede suspenso,*" an ignorant card-marker had drawn the figure suspended by his foot instead of standing, and this has been copied by others. It may be that the words used in cribbage to-day "Two for his heels," may have come down to us from four hundred years ago in connection with this Atout card of "Le Pendu." See Fig. 25.

Fig. 23. 19th Century.

Fig. 24
18th Century.

No. XIII. Death.

There are some variations in the way this 13th Atout is represented, but generally he is shown as a skeleton with a scythe mowing off the heads of kings, queens, rich and poor. None can escape his terrible scythe. He is sometimes shown as a rider on a white horse, and on others on a black horse. It is significant that for some hundreds of years in all European countries the number thirteen has been associated with bad luck, misfortune, sorrow and death, and the No. 13 on the Atout cards invariably illustrates death. On a pack in the *Bibliotheque Nationale* it is shown as a skeleton on a black horse with uplifted scythe, slashing at a number of Kings, Cardinals, Bishops, etc. Fig. 26.

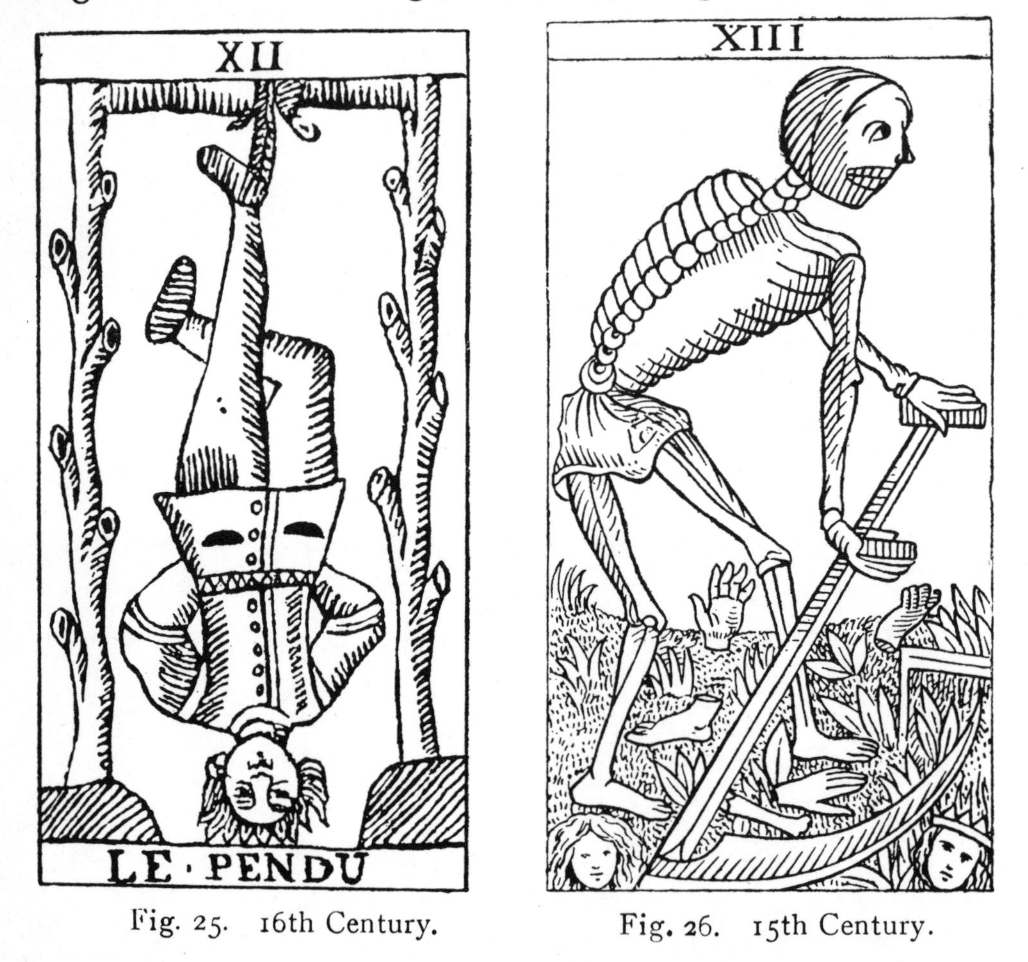

Fig. 25. 16th Century.

Fig. 26. 15th Century.

In a French book on games, published at Paris by Etienne Layson in 1668, it is said that the Swiss and Germans prefer *Tarocca* to any other game, and after describing the cards, the Author mentions various methods of playing with them. In one game called *Triomphe forcée*, five cards are dealt to each player, and the one who is fortunate enough to hold the *Fool* (*Juggler*) takes up what he has staked upon the game. The holder of *La Force* (Atout No. 11) takes up twice as much, and the holder of Atout No. 13, which is *Death* (*La Morte*) ultimately sweeps the board in spite of all attempts to prevent it.

Fig. 27. 18th Century.

No. XIIII. Temperance.

A female with wings, who is pouring a liquid from one vase into another, is shown in Fig. 27. This may refer to making an oblation to the gods, by pouring wine or oil before them, as that was one of the earliest methods of consulting the gods, and is said to have been used by the Babylonians at least 2000 B.C. It represents temperance, health, production, economy, and offspring. It will be seen the name is spelt "Tenperance" on this old 18th Century Atout.

No. XV. The Devil.

Generally the 15th Atout is represented by Typhon and is shown as a ferocious looking nude figure seated, his right hand raised, and a burning torch in his left hand. His feet have long, ugly claws, and on his head two long, curved horns are fixed. Two wings proceed from his shoulders and a reversed pentagram is on his forehead between the two horns. In front of him stand a nude man and woman chained together, the end of the chain being fastened to the rock on which he is sitting. These are analagous with those on No. 6, as if representing Adam and Eve *after* the fall. Figs. 28 & 29.

Fig. 29 taken from an old Italian pack of the early 17th century shows the same idea as Fig. 28, but in place of the man and woman, two small devils are chained.

Fig. 28. 19th Century.

Fig. 29. 17th Century.

No. XVI. The Tower.

This Atout card shows a high tower which has been struck by lightning, the top being broken away and falling amid flames which are issuing from the opening, while from the windows two men are shown being hurled to the ground. This no doubt refers to the legend recorded by the Greek historian Herodotus, the father of history, who was born in the year 484 B.C. He tells us that the Pharoah Rameses II ordered a tower to be constructed to contain his treasure, but in spite of the fact that he alone possessed a key of the tower, he found that his valuables were constantly disappearing, although there was only one door. He therefore caused a watch to be set, and soon found that two of the sons of the architect could gain admission by removing a large stone that had been left loose for the purpose of thieving, and when the two men discovered that they were found out, they threw themselves headlong down from the top of the tower. In some Tarot packs this card (No. xvi) is called "*La Maison Dieu,*" and again the "Castle of Plutus" the Roman god of wealth who is said to have been deprived of his sight by Zeus, so that he might distribute his gifts blindly and without any regard to merit. Again, some think it represents the destruction of the temples of Babylon. It stands for vice, destruction, sorrow, and all that is bad and wicked. (Fig. 30).

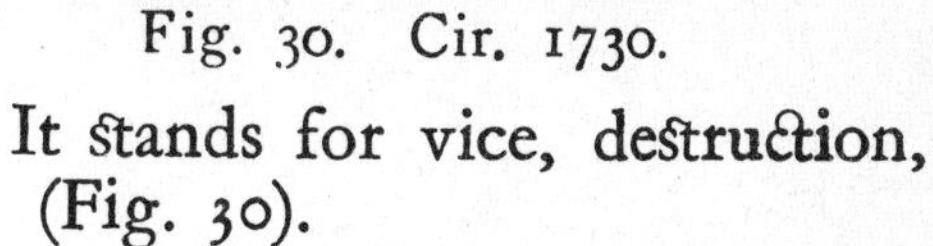

Fig. 30. Cir. 1730.

No. XVII. The Star.

This shows a young, nude woman kneeling by a river and pouring liquids from two vessels. Above her are usually seven stars or planets and a great radiant star (*l'etoile flamboyante*). She may be intended to represent Hebe, the Goddess of Youth, who is said to have waited upon the gods and filled their cups with nectar. Tradition says she had the power of making aged persons young again. In the very oldest pack of Atout cards there was a gazelle standing beside her, but this is omitted in the more modern packs. Creation, song, speech, music, hope, immortality, eternal youth, and beauty are typified by this Atout. In this illustration of No. XVII Atout (*See Fig.* 31). there are only five-pointed stars.

Fig. 31. 15th Century

No. XVIII. The Moon.

A full moon, with rays of light issuing from it, is shown on this card, and below are two strong towers, one on either side. Two dogs (sometimes a dog and a wolf) are barking at the moon, and a cray-fish crawls from a river on to the land. The card signifies an aim, an end, and shows our lower animal nature, types of which are represented below—the dog and wolf and that which comes out of the depths. Fig. 32. See also Fig. 171.

Fig. 32. 16th Century. Fig. 33. 19th Century.

No. XIX. The Sun.

A representation of the Sun in full splendour is shown at the top of this Atout, and below in front of a wall a naked child is sometimes represented seated on a white horse and holding a large red banner. Over the wall are some large sunflowers. On another pack the horse and child are replaced by a young man and woman who are holding each other by the hand and appear to be lovers. The sun has always been looked upon as a god and this Atout card would represent an awaking excitement and a happy marriage. (Fig. 33).

No. XX. The last Judgement.

Here we see an angel emerging from a cloud and blowing a trumpet, while below the graves are opening and the dead are shown coming forth, a man on the left, a woman on the right, and their child between them. It represents movement, originality and regeneration, and is said to be dedicated to Pluto,* the giver of wealth. The design of the angel blowing a trumpet is a common one on many 17th and 18th century tombstones. See Fig. 34.

Fig. 34. 18th Century

Fig. 35. 16th Century.

No. XXI. The World.

Within an elliptical wreath of laurel leaves, this card shows a woman quite nude except for a thin flowing veil. She is carrying a

* Pluto the brother of Jupiter and Neptune, also called Hades the God of the Nether World.

Plate 1.

Plate 5.

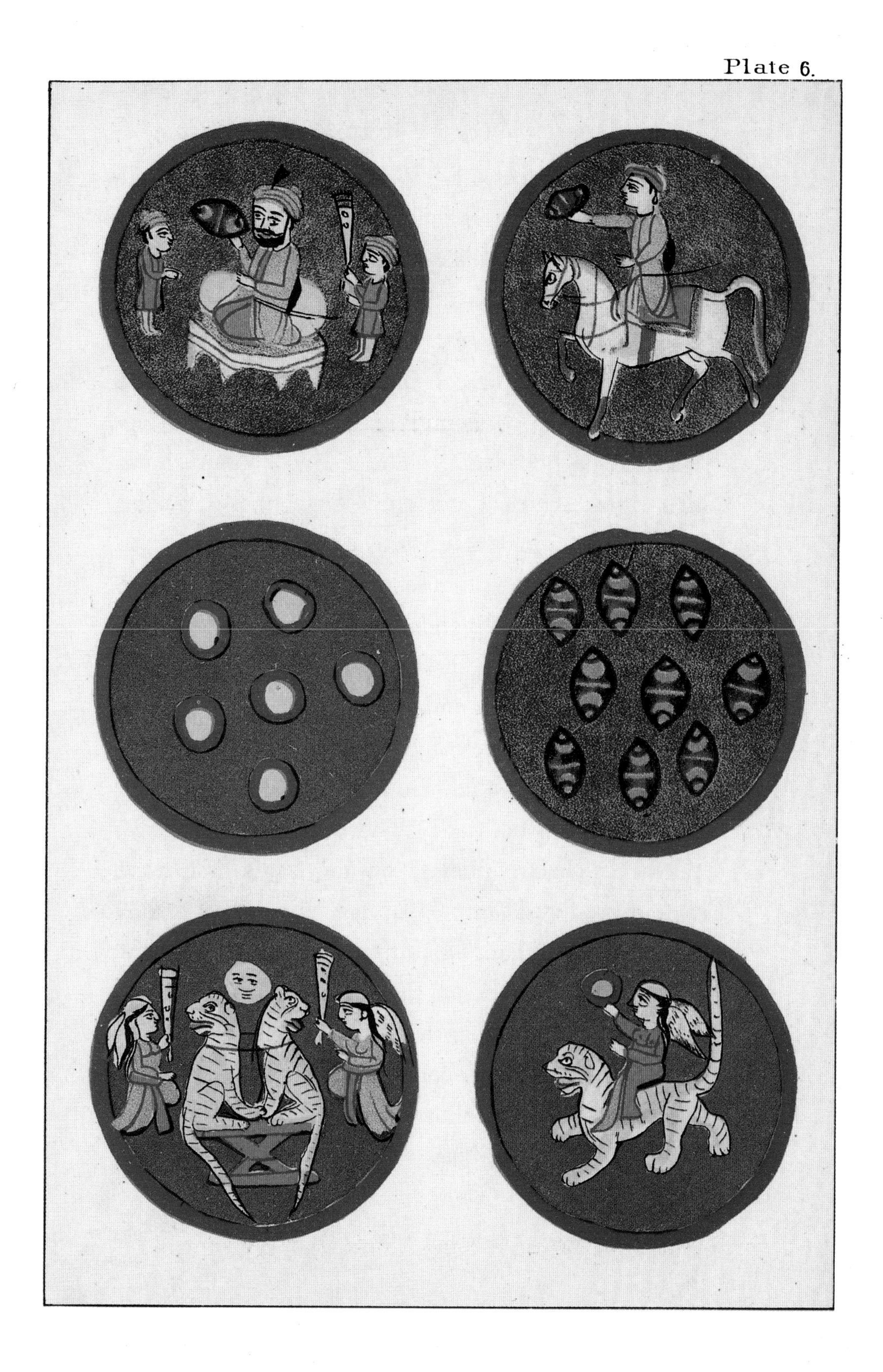

Plate 7.

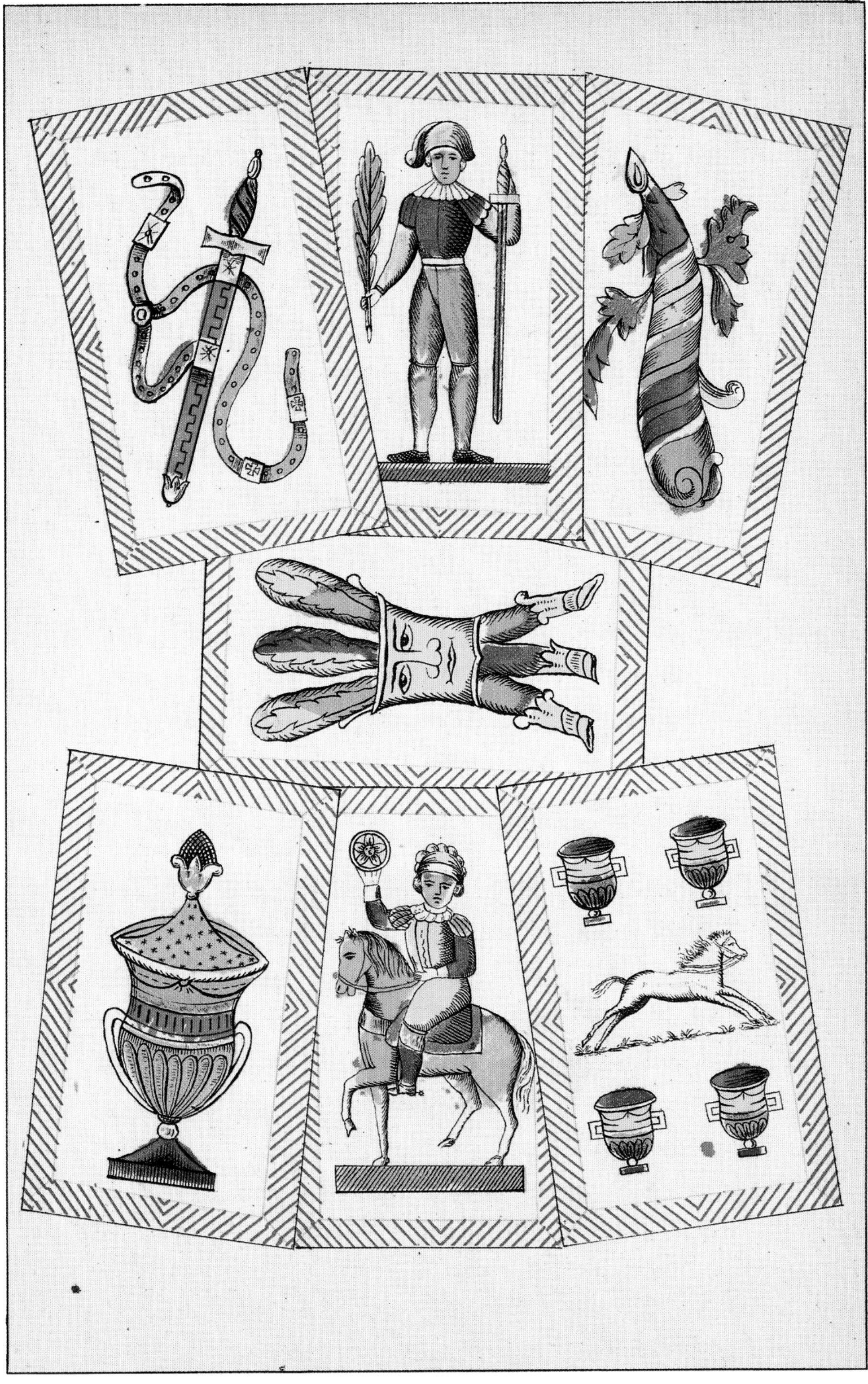

Plate 8.

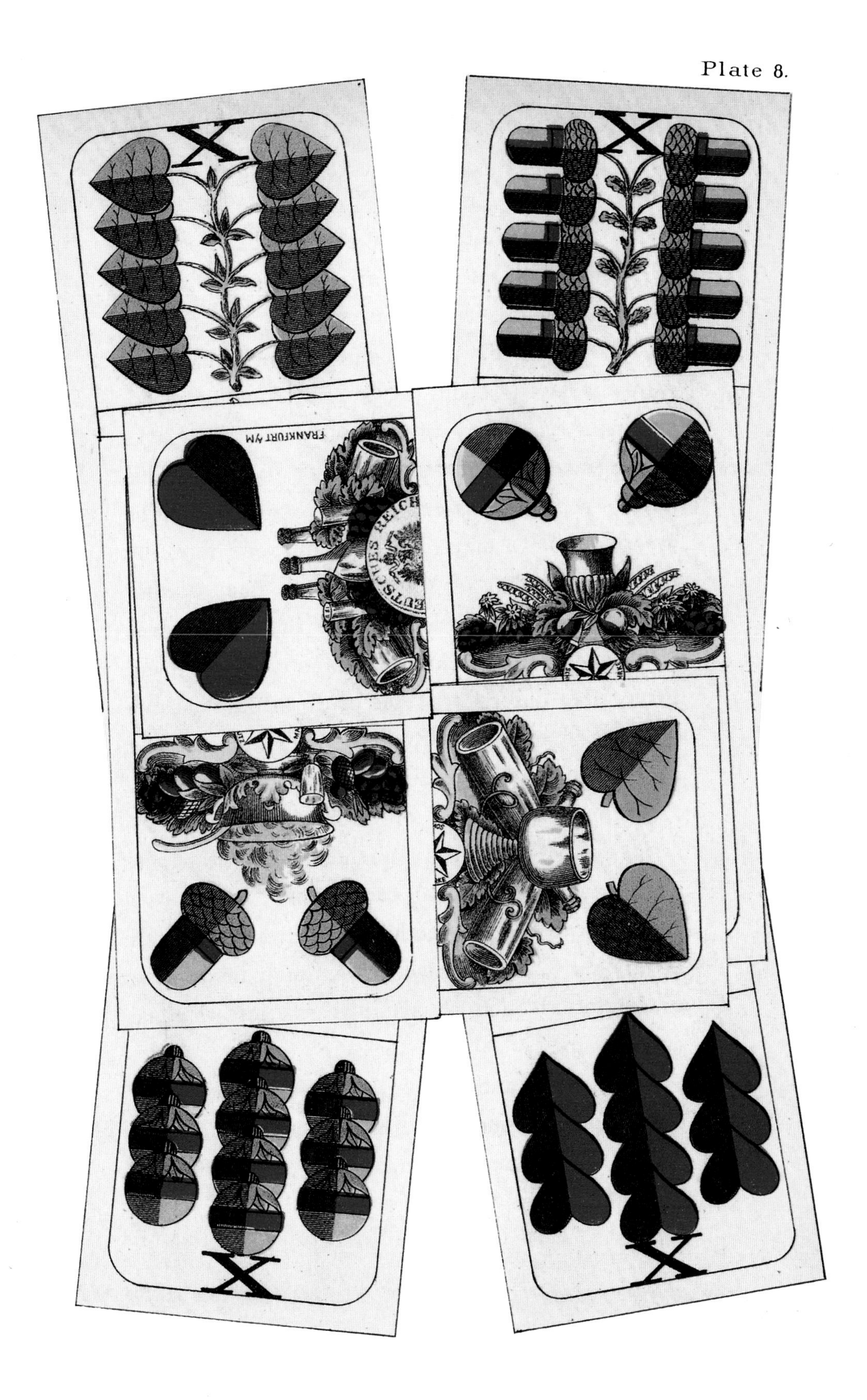

Plate 9.

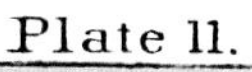
Plate 11.

lancelot

hogier

valery : F :

Rolant

SIR JEFFERY AMHERST's Compliments to Mrs Paul Miller

and desires the Favour of her Company to a Ball, at the New Assembly Room, on Saturday the 23d Instant, being the Anniversary of St. George.

Head-Quarters, April 18, 1763.

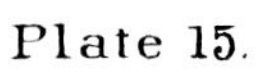
Plate 15.

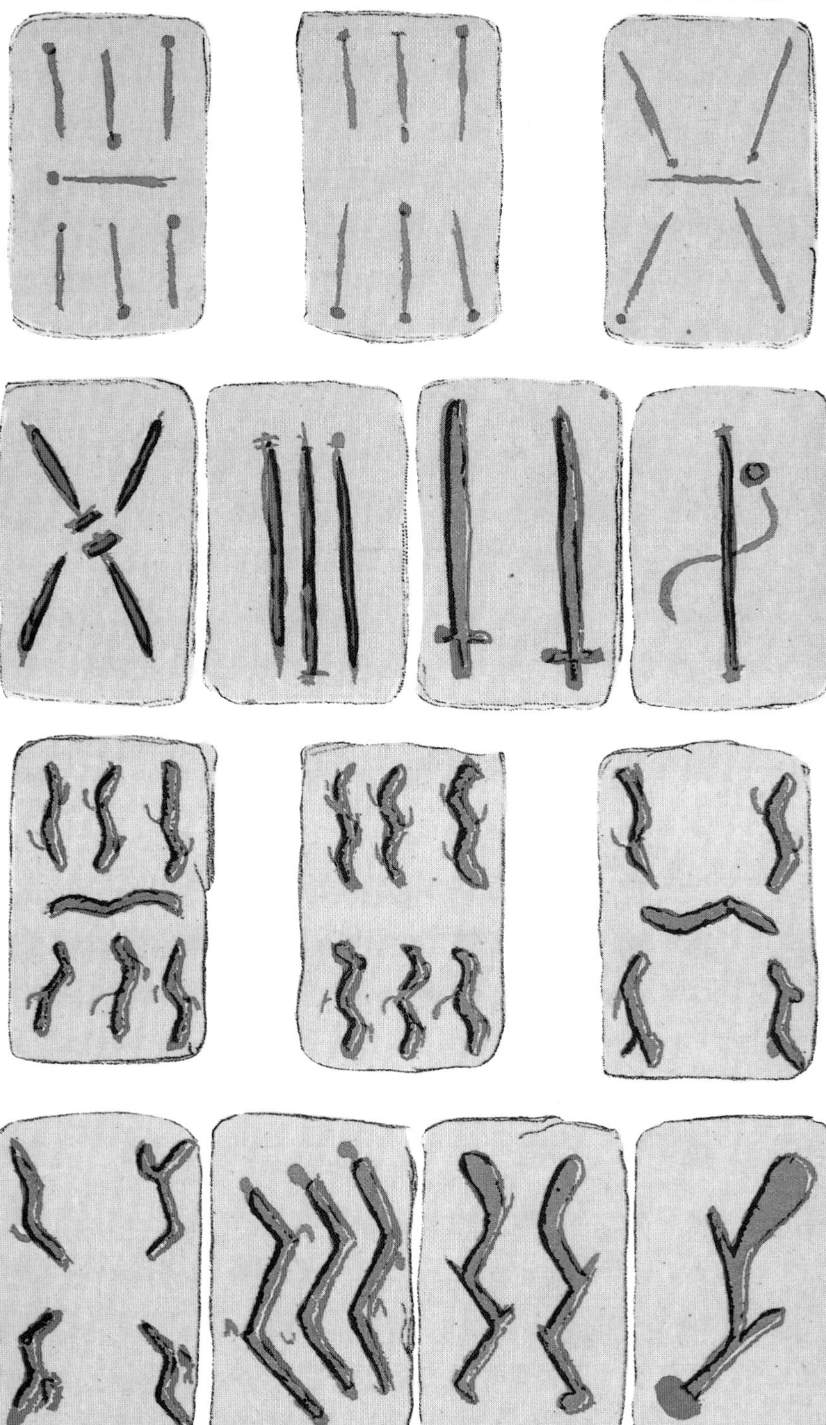

Plate 16.

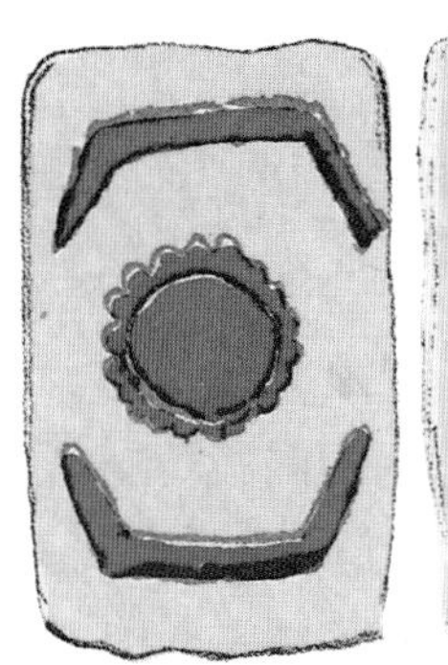

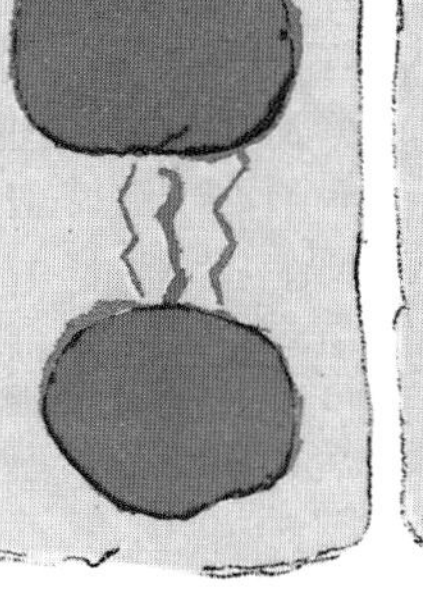

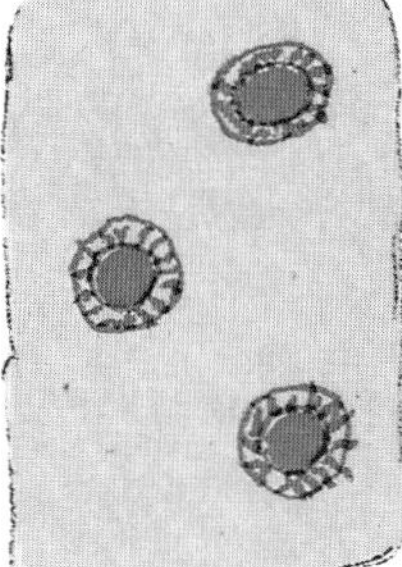

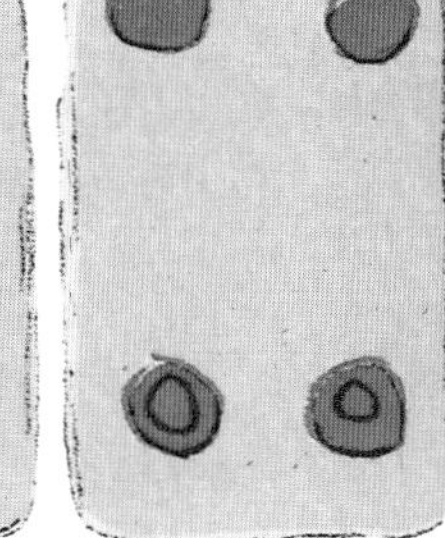

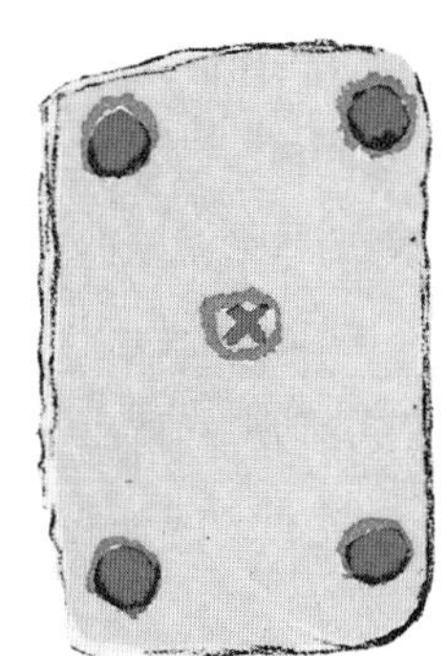

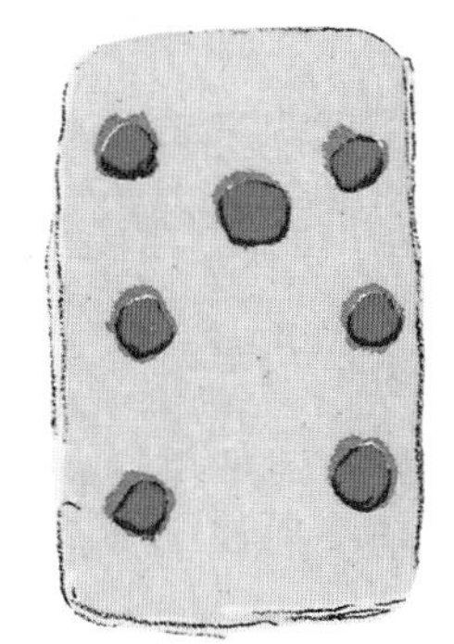

Plate 17.

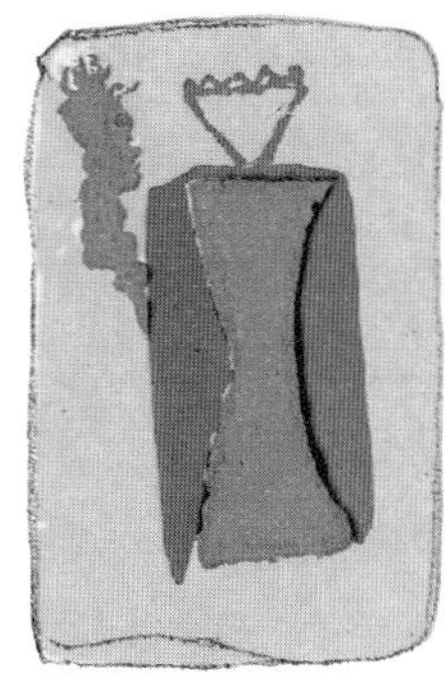

Plate 21.

Plate 22.

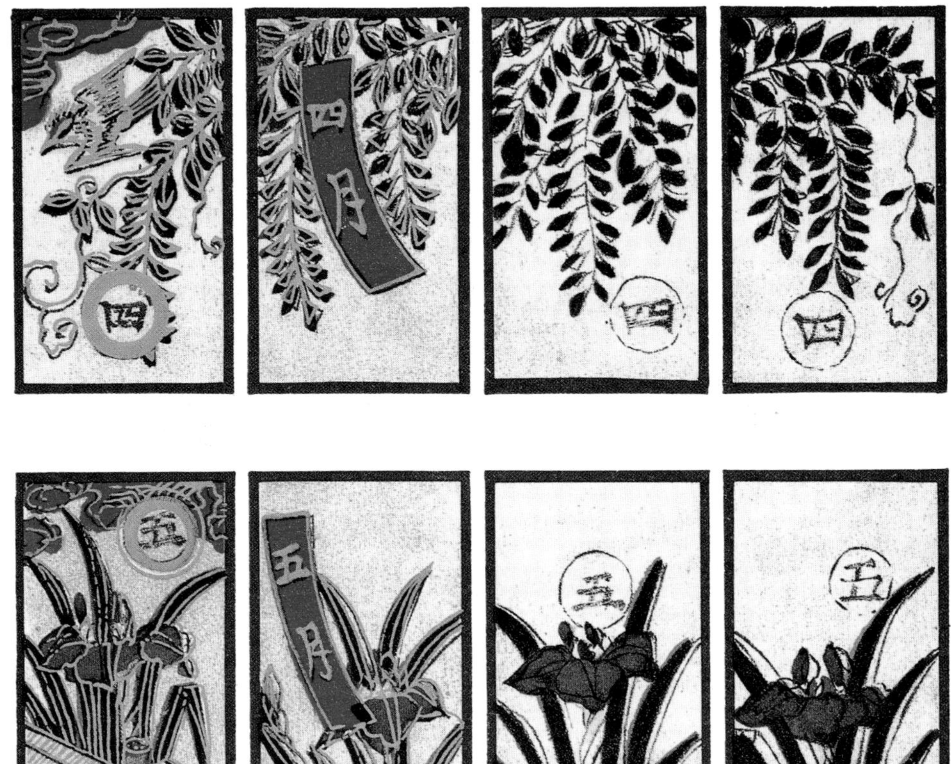

七
七
七
八
八
八
八
九
九
九
九月

Plate 24

wand, probably representing the wand or caduceus of Aaron. In the four corners are the emblems of the evangelists, which one writer states St. John borrowed from Ezekiel, who copied them from Assyria and Babylon. They show the man, or an angel, the eagle, the ox and the lion, and may also suggest the four suits as well as the four seasons.

1. The Man signifies knowledge and mystery, also Winter.
2. The Eagle signifies inspiration, also Spring.
3. The Ox signifies strength, also Autumn.
4. The Lion signifies courage, also Summer.

These four figures are also said to represent the four elementary forms of the Kabbalah; the four metals, and also the four mysterious letters of the *Tora** of the Jews, of the wheels of Ezekiel,† *Rota,* and of the *Tarot,* which, according to Postel is the key of the things hidden from the beginning of the world.

It represents success, marriage, contentment and truth.

The Fool

This Atout has no number upon it, and is called *Le Fou, Il Matto,* or the Joker. The Italian name is said to be derived from an Egyptian one—Mat, signifying perfection—it also represents Mercury as the staff and purse are the attributes of that god. *Le Fou* is shown walking with light step, and with his bundle suggests a pedlar or a merchant. In some of the older Italian packs he is shown naked or with very tattered garments, while in Austria he is dressed in parti-coloured clothes as a harlequin or jester, and is supposed to be the symbol of folly, frivolity, or chance. In play he dominates every card in the pack.

The whole of these twenty-two Atout cards would seem to express, in illustrations, the life of a young man, the many things that go to make up human life, such as love, religion, friendship, uncertainty, ambition, luck, marriage, illness, hope, despair, enemies, and death.

* Fig. 12. † Ezekiel, Chap. I, Verses 10 to 20

"These mystic Cards would lift the veil, and bid us take a look within,
They show us Love, Ambition, Hope, with Marriage, Luck, Despair and Sin,
Pope, Empress, Justice, Temperance, even Death who mows down all,
Showing our life is but a dream, a breath, whose scythe on all must fall."

These packs of 78 cards, viz., 56 Tarots and 22 Atouts, are still used in Italy and some writers contend that the rules of the game known as "The Man" suggest that originally they were used probably more for fortune-telling purposes than as an amusement, and the superstitious people conceived they were receiving divine guidance when consulting these cards. Even in our own day there are many who secretly believe in the power of the cards to help them to look into the future.

Fig. 36.

18th Century

Fig. 37. 16th Century.

ASIATIC PLAYING CARDS.

Chinese.

Playing cards have been known in China from very early times, and the Chinese quote from their own authors as proof of the long pedigree of the game. The game of Teen-tsze-pae, or dotted cards was, it is said, invented for the amusement of the wives of the Emperor Seun-ho, who ascended the throne in 1131. Some, however, say that cards first came from Hindostan, and that the Chinese simply changed the types.*

Fig. 38.

It has always been said of the Chinese that they are a gambling nation, and in Fig. 38 we have an illustration showing a game of cards in progress, copied from Breitkopf, the German writer on playing cards, who says he copied it from an old Chinese work of which it formed the title page.

* page 20.

The Chinese cards differ in shape and size from those of other nations. They are long and very narrow. The five cards shown (see Fig. 39), are from two different packs. The sizes of the actual cards illustrated are $3\frac{3}{4}$ in. by $\frac{5}{8}$ in., and $3\frac{3}{4}$ in. by 1 in.

Nos. 1 and 2 are the one of the suit of chains, Nos. 3 and 4 are the three and four of the suit of cakes.

They are printed in black on a white ground, and four cards of the pack are overprinted in red.

Fig. 39.

The general name for cards in China is *Che-pae,* signifying "paper tickets." A pack of dotted cards consists of 32 pieces. Ten of these are classed in pairs, the first pair, called *Che-tsun* (the most honourable) being superior to all the others. These may be considered as court cards, as the one depicts the figure of a man and the other that of a woman.

The second pair are called *Tien-pae* (celestial cards), the third pair *Te-pae* (terrestial cards), the fourth pair *Tin-pae* (human cards), and the fifth pair *Ho-pae.*

The cards most commonly used are called *Tseen-wan-che-pae* (a thousand times ten thousand) and the pack of 30 is divided into three suits of nine cards each, and three single cards which are superior to all the others. One suit is *Kew-ko-wan,* that is, "The nine ten thousands," or myriads of Kwan, which are strings of shells, beads, or money.

Another is called *Kew-ho-so* (nine units of chains), and a third *Kew-ho-ping* (nine units of cakes.) The names of the three single cards are:

Tseen-wan	A thousand times ten thousand.
Hung-hwa	The red flower.
Pih-hwa	The white flower.*

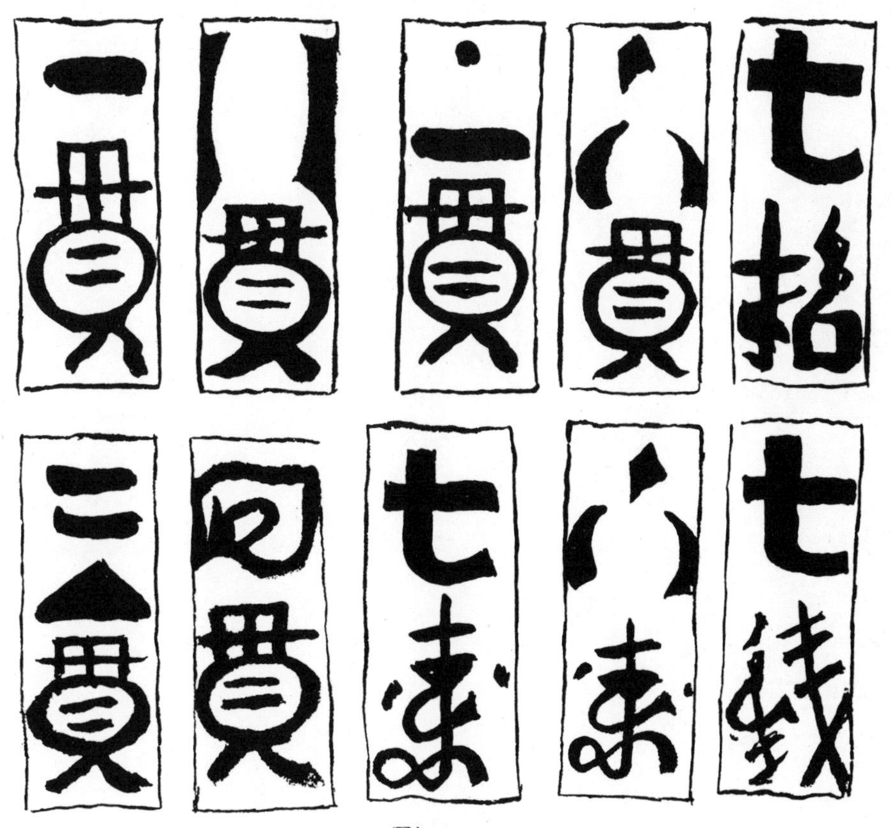

Fig. 40.

Another variety of cards has the same name as Chinese chess—*Ken-ma-paon* (chariots, horses and guns). This would seem to corroborate what has been suggested as to the probability of the game of cards having originally come from the game of chess.† Again, all the ancient packs had chequered backs and the backs of the oldest Tarot cards retain this resemblance and some writers have decided that "Tarot" means chequered.

The Chinese name for a single card is *Shen* (a fan), and may mean the "fanning" out of the cards when playing.

* Devil's Picture Books, page 66. † page 19.

Hindostani.

There is no doubt that cards were known in India at a very early date. Mr. Singer describes a splendid pack of Hindoo cards and reproduces many of them. They are painted on ivory. The backs are gilded and they number 96.

Fig. 41.

Fig. 42.

Fig. 43.

Fig. 44.

Fig. 45.

Fig. 46.

Mr. Chatto also describes a pack of Hindostanee cards which, he says, are in the possession of the Royal Asiatic Society. These consist of 10 suits of 12 cards=120, and the marks of the suits are the ten emblems of the ten Avators, or incarnations of Vichnou.

A pack which I have in my collection (see page 61) consists of eight suits of twelve cards (numerals 1 to 10 and a King and a Vizier)=96, and the colours and marks on the various suits are as follows :—

1. Dark brown spot with white dot on yellow ground.
2. Gold spot with red ring on green ground.
3. Green and yellow darts on red ground.
4. Red and gold birds on dark green ground.
5. Black baskets on red ground.
6. Men with red turbans on yellow ground.
7. Green spots with red banks on dark brown ground.
8. Gold and yellow spots on black ground.

On Nos. 1, 3, 4, 5, 7 and 8 the King is seated on a throne; on No. 2 on a tiger, and on No. 6 on an elephant. On Nos. 1 and 8 the Vizier is on a black horse, on Nos. 3, 5 and 7 on a white horse, on No. 2 on a tiger, on No. 4 on a camel, on No. 6 on a bull. Figs. 64, 65, 66.

These cards are circular and slightly less than 1¾ inches diameter.

Another pack of circular cards in my collection consists of 10 suits, each of 12 cards=120. These are 3¼ inches in diameter and beautifully lacquered and finished in *very* brilliant colours. Figs. 47 and 48. Each suit consists of a King and Vizier and numerals 1 to 10.

Description of the Ten Kings.

WILD BOARS on dark green ground.

The King is shown as a man with a boar's head and four arms (?) and he is standing on a man who is lying on the ground.

BATTLE AXES on yellow ground.

The King is shown with 26 arms and with 3 lying at his feet. He is attended by a slave who holds a large axe.

VASES on orange ground.

A slave is handing a vase to the King who is seated on his throne with his Queen at his side. Two officers and a female slave are also in attendance.

Fig. 47, Vizier of Goats.

Fig. 48, King of Fish.

Fig. 49, King of Horses.

Fig. 50, Eight of Monkeys.

HORSES on crimson ground.

A figure is standing in front of a white horse, Fig. 49, and holding a large baton in his hand. A halo of gold radiations is around his head.

FISHES on black ground.

A black King with four arms is issuing from the mouth of a large fish. Two officers are behind him and the figure of a demon(?) or imp is seated before him on a large white shell. Fig. 48.

MONKEYS on red ground.

The King with his Queen beside him, is seated upon his throne. Two monkeys are sitting in front of him and two officers in full dress are behind him. Figure 50 shows the 8 of Monkeys.

TORTOISES on maroon ground.

The King seems to be issuing from the mouth of a large tortoise. Two officers are behind him and in front is the figure of a demon (?) seated on a large white shell.

LOTUS FLOWERS (?) on orange ground.

The King is shown as a figure with four arms seated upon a throne under an umbrella.

GOATS on red ground.

The King is standing under a large tree with two birds near it. He is attended by four female figures.
Fig. 47 shows the Vizier of Goats.

LIONS on green ground.

Shows the King with a lion's face seated upon a pedestal. He has four arms with two of which he seems to be killing or tearing the body of a black monkey or child which he is holding on his knees. A man and a woman stand, one on either side, and the man, with hands clasped, seems to be praying for mercy for the figure on the King's lap.

Description of the various Kings on the ten suits.

On Nos. 1, 2, 3, 8 and 10 the Kings are White men, and on Nos. 4, 5, 6, 7 and 9 they are Black men. All the Viziers are shown on horseback, the horses being of various colours, and on each a slave is seen holding an umbrella. Fig. 47.

Nos. 1 and 10 are red horses; No. 2 brown; No. 3 black; Nos. 4, 5 and 9 white; Nos. 6 and 7 yellow; No. 8 blue.

The Ten Suits would seem to represent the Ten *Avators of Vichnou* (Vishnu) one of the three principal deities in the Hindoo religion. With slight exceptions these ten Avators of Vichnou are generally given in the following order:—

The Fish.	The Lion.	The Goat.
The Tortoise.	The Monkey.	The Booth.
The Wild Boar.	The Battle Axe.	The Horse.
	The Bow.(?)	

Dr. Hunter, in the "Dictionary, Hindoostanee and English," mentions a pack composed of 96 cards divided into 8 suits. In each suit are two Court Cards, the King and the Wuzeer (Vizier) and ten cards, numbered 1 to 10. Four suits are termed superior and four inferior, and the names of the suits are given as follows:—

Taj . . .	a crown.
Soofed . . .	a white or silver coin, figuratively, the moon.
Shumsher . .	a sabre.
Gholam . . .	a slave.
Chung . . .	a harp.
Soorkh . . .	a red or gold coin, figuratively, the sun.
Burat . . .	a royal diploma.
Quimash . . .	merchandise.

The tradition regarding the origin of the Hindoostanee cards is that they were invented by a favourite wife to wean her husband from a qad habit he had acquired of pulling out his beard.

As the marks on the Spanish and Italian suits are supposed to represent the four principal classes of men in Europe, viz.:—

1. Cups or Chalices, the Churchmen.
2. Swords, the Soldiers.
3. Money, the Merchants.
4. Clubs or Batons, the Workmen.

so it is just as easy to see a parallel in the four superior suits of the Indian cards, viz.:—

1. Taj, a crown, Royalty.
2. Shumsher, a sword, Soldiers.
3. Soofed, silver money, Merchants.
4. Gholam, a slave, Workers.

These again can be traced in the four great historical castes of the Hindoos:—

1. Brahmins—priests.
2. Vais yas—tradesmen and artificers.
3. Chetryas—soldiers.
4. Sudras—slaves and lowest class of labourers.

Figs. 41 to 46 illustrate six from a very beautiful pack of Hindoo cards, painted on Ivory and finished with all the delicacy of miniature paintings. There are seven suits, SUNS, represented by gold discs, MOONS, on silver discs, SWORDS, HARPS, CROWNS or TURBANS, CUSHIONS, and LETTERS. Each of these seven suits consists of ten numerals with two Royal or Court cards, which appear to represent a King and a Vizier.

These six cards illustrated probably represent the King of CROWNS or TURBANS Fig. 41, the Vizier of CUSHIONS seated on a camel, Fig. 42, the Vizier of LETTERS seated on a White Horse, Fig. 43, who is offering a letter written in black on a silver ground, the Vizier of MOONS on a leopard, Fig. 44, the Vizier of SWORDS on a horse, Fig. 45 and one of the cards from the suit of SUNS, Fig. 46.

Besides these eighty-four there are twelve other cards, apparently of no definite suit, but on which are groups of figures, some male and some female.*

Fig. 51.

Fig. 51 (half size) shows four Viziers—Suns, Birds, Letters and Cushions— from a circular pack of 96.

Japanese.

Playing cards as used by the Japanese are among the most interesting, as they are also the most dainty, and are quite different from the Chinese, Hindostanee, or Persian. They are unique both in the symbols used and in the fact that they do not seem to have been influenced in any way by the devices used by other nations. Although the same shape as those used in Europe, they are much smaller, being only 2¼ in. by 1¼ in. in size. They are painted and lacquered and must be very awkward to play with. There are 49 cards made up of 12 suits of 4 cards each, and also a plain white card which would seem to be the same as our

* Singer, page 16.

"Joker." The 12 suits represent the 12 months of the year and on the cards are painted flowers, trees and emblems as follows :—

January .	Pine trees, on one of which is a large white stork.
February	Plum blossom.
March .	Red Cherry.
April .	Wisteria. Fig. 52.
May .	Iris. Fig. 53.
June .	Large red peonies, on one card are two butterflies.
July .	Large spiked leaves, on one card a deer.
August .	Four mountains with long grass ; one card with three birds on it.
September	Red and yellow chrysanthemums.
October .	Red and green leaves, on one card a boar. Fig. 54.
November	Willow trees. On two cards falling rain is depicted, on another a bird is seen in addition to the trees, and on a fourth a man with an umbrella. Fig. 55.
December	The Imperial Plant. On one card a pheasant in full plumage.

A game played by the Japanese is called "Huzuki Fuda" (The Winter Cherry Game). Each suit is composed of four cards of the numerals 1 to 10, and an extra card (a horned goblin's head) which probably acts as a "Joker", there is also a plain white card. The Aces and Tens are indicated by large characters, the suits of the other numerals by balls of the number required. Fig. 56.

Another game called "Mekuri Fuda" (Turn over Pack), consists of 41 cards composed of four cards of each of the numerals 1 to 10 and an extra card, showing an illustration of the Japanese Emperor seated.

The Aces have an ornamental ground, the suit marks up to 9 are crossed diagonal bars and are numbered, and the tenth is a double-ended figure holding up a square marked with a cross.

This pack is said to be used mostly for gambling. Fig. 57.

Japanese.

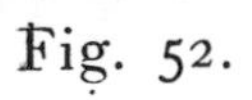

Fig. 52.

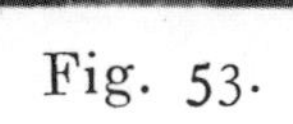

Fig. 53.

Fig. 54

Fig. 55.

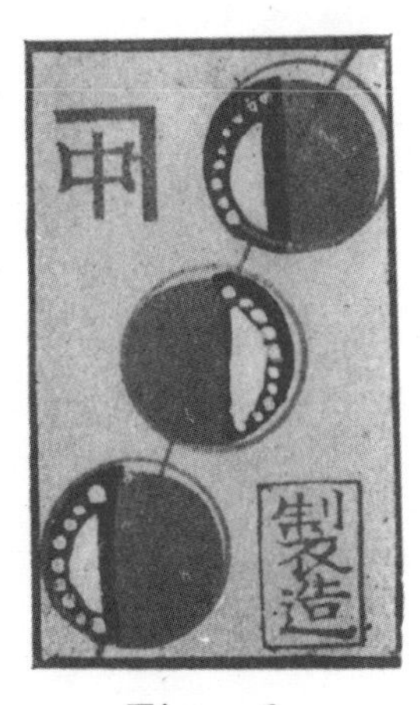

Fig. 56.

Fig, 57.

Burmese.

Fig. 58.

Fig 59.

Fig. 60.

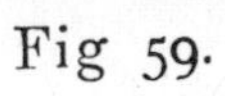

Burmese.

I cannot give many particulars of the cards used by the Burmese, as I have only part of a pack in my collection.

While there is a resemblance in the shape to the Japanese cards, and those used in Europe, the devices upon them are very much like the Persian and Indian. Each has an ornamental border and canopy, and is 2¼ in. by 1¾ in. in size. These cards were used by the Rajpoot Tribe.

In Fig. 58, we have a vizier with an animal's head, seated upon a white horse, and attended by two slaves. The Kings are seated upon thrones, attended by two slaves, one of whom holds an umbrella. Fig. 60, One of the numeral cards, Fig. 59, shows the eight of monkeys.

Tibetan.

These are hand-painted on canvas and scarcely seem to merit the name of cards. They are 2¼ in. by 2¾ in. and have various designs drawn in fine black lines and filled in with rather brilliant colours.

The Director and Secretary of the Victoria and Albert Museum reports on these cards as follows :—

"Dear Sir, 6 November, 1926.

I beg to inform you that the cards which you send are Tibetan playing cards, each bearing well-known symbols, emblems and devices, and they seem to have been made about the beginning of the last century. They were possibly used for fortune-telling."

Yours faithfully,

Eric Maclagan, *Director & Secretary.*

A Tibetan gentleman who examined some of these cards said they were used by the priests in their religious services, a card being placed in a cleft stick, which in turn is fixed in a little heap of clay or a vessel filled with grains of salt. He stated that there were many such cards in Tibet, but they were not used for fortune-telling, and he gave the following explanations of some of them. Nos. 2, 11, 13, 18 and 22 are pictures of Deities. No. 4 shows a tray filled with precious stones. No. 16 a golden wheel, No. 20 an elephant with a precious gem on its back, Fig. 68. No. 24 a precious stone between two golden fishes, and No. 27 a conch shell. Fig. 68 is one of the Deities.

Persian. ?

Fig. 61.

Fig. 62.

Fig. 63.

Hindostanee.

Fig. 64.

Fig. 65.

Fig. 66.

Fig. 67.

Fig. 68.

Tibetan.

ITALIAN CARDS.

Fig. 69.

These four cards from an Italian Tarot pack show the Ace of Swords, Queen of Batons, King of Cups, and the Atout No. 13, Doath, who is shown with his scythe. They date from about 1790.

Fig. 70.

The three cards, Fig. 70, are from an old Italian pack of Tarot cards, which date from 1500–1520. The first one, showing an angel standing upon a crescent moon, seems to represent the Queen of Money The middle one shows a cup at the bottom, while above a woman representing the Queen of Cups is bathing. The third card shows the Knave of Cups.

Fabb Dotti, Milano.

The King of Spades, shown in Fig. 71, belongs to a pack of 52 cards published at Milan by "*Fabb Dotti, Milano.*" The suit signs are Clubs, Diamonds, Hearts and Spades and the coat cards are beautifully engraved and coloured.

The pips on the numerals are printed from stencils and are arranged on the cards all the same way, none are reversed.

They are printed on vellum paper, which is turned over from the back, forming a border, and the word "MILANO" is worked into the design on the back of each card. On the King of Hearts the papal arms are stamped with the words F.I.—C.40.—LOMBARDI underneath, and the maker's name is also on this card.

Fig. 71.

The figures on the coat cards are all full length, and dressed in most elaborate costumes. The four Kings and Queens are all crowned.

The Queen of Diamonds holds a red rose, and the Queen of Clubs is holding the sacred heart from which proceeds a bright yellow flame. The four Valets have heraldic devices embroidered upon their doublets.

The size, $3\frac{3}{4}$ in. by 2 in., is somewhat unusual.

Trappola Cards, cir. 1550.

The first game which seems to have been known to the Italians was "Trappola," and it was played with a pack of 36 cards. The four Suits were Swords, Cups or Chalices, Money or Rings, and Batons or Sticks. Each suit consisted of three Coat cards and six numerals, viz.: King, Knight, and Servant and the 1, 2, 7, 8, 9 and 10=36.

On page 65 six cards are illustrated which are taken from an early Italian Trappola pack.‡

Fig. 73.	Nine of Cups.	Fig. 76.	Six of Batons.
Fig. 74.	Knight of Batons.	Fig. 77.	King of Cups.
Fig. 75.	Nine of Money or Rings.	Fig. 78.	Seven of Swords.

Singer, who illustrates these six cards, says they were found in the covers of an old book, and date from about 1550.

It is interesting to note how the three Coat cards, King, Knight and Servant, correspond with the German King, Obermann and Untermann, as used in Germany to-day.

Another very interesting point is the fact that the four suit signs are identical with four symbols which are held in the four hands of "ARDHANARI," a composite deity of India, of whom the left half is "SHIVA" and the right half "DURGA."*

* Fig. 311. ‡ Singer page 199.

Introduction into Europe.

Although it is uncertain into which European country playing cards were first introduced, some of the oldest cards known are found in Italy and are mentioned as being in common use in the 13th century, and in a manuscript dated 1299 they are expressly mentioned.

If, however, the games mentioned in the record of the Council of Worcester, (see page 22) refer to playing cards, then England can claim priority.

Early Italian Trappola Playing Cards

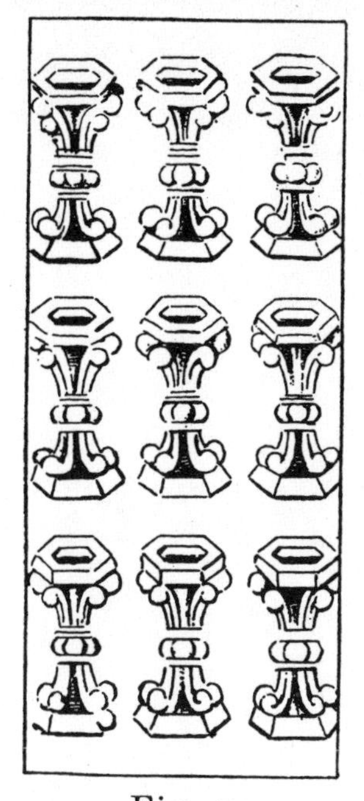

Fig. 73.

Fig. 74.

Fig. 75.

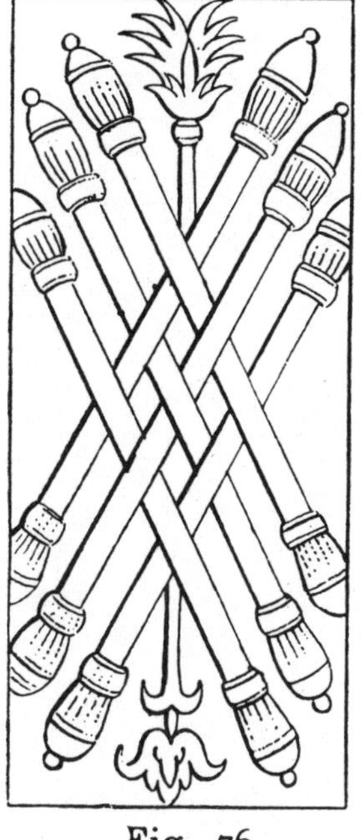

Fig. 76.

Fig. 77.

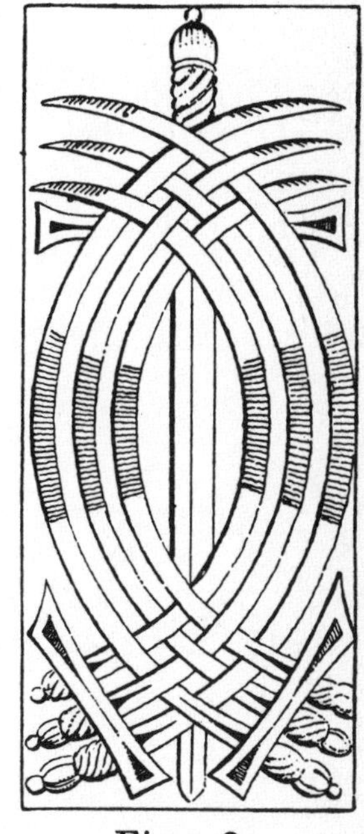

Fig. 78.

Singer page 199.

Tarrochi Cards, XV. century.

In the "Exhibition of Italian Art" held at Burlington House, London, in January 1930 some very beautifully finished cards were on view. They were parts of two packs of the XVth Century.

Thirty-two Tarocchi Cards of the XVth Century

Lent by the HEIRS OF DUKE VISCONTI DI MODRONE, MILAN.

Part of a set of sixty-seven Tarocchies, which were illuminated between 1428 and 1447 for Filippo Maria Visconti, who is seen on one of them holding the hand of his Duchess, Maria of Savoy, with their arms on a pavilion in the background. The backgrounds of the cards carrying figures are diapered gold; the rest have silver backgrounds.

Each card. 7½ in. by 3¾ in.

Have been in the Visconti family since executed.

Sixteen Tarocchi Cards of the XVth Century

Lent by SIGNORA FRIEDA BRAMBILLA AND DAUGHTERS AND BY SIGNORA JULIA BRAMBILLA.

Cards illuminated with the personnel of a pack of cards with gold diapered backgrounds; others with non-figure subjects and with silver background. Those above were probably illuminated for Filippo Maria Visconti, as several of them bear his motto: *A bon droit.*

Each card. 6¾ in. by 2¾ in.

These cards are almost identical with Fig. 170, which is a facsimile of "The Emperor" Atout, No. IV. one of the cards from the set described on page 115.

Fig. 79 is a copy of an old print engraved by Israel Van Mecken about the year 1495. It is taken from the frontispiece in Singer's "*Researches into the History of Playing Cards and Origin of Printing*," and is one of a set, by the same artist, which depicts various scenes in domestic life. It is interesting as affording proof that cards were well known in the 15th century, and it also gives an idea of the costume of the period. The shoes, with the long pointed toes, denominated *poulains* by the French, show that the players are persons of fashion. The lady appears to have turned up the winning card, to the great surprise of the gentleman.

Fig. 79.

GERMAN CARDS.

Old Bohemian Legend.

It has been suggested that the first European playing cards owed their origin to an old Bohemian legend which still exists in varied forms. This legend tells of one Rubezahl, or Karl as his name became in the German version, who watches for travellers with his turnips and his jug of water on the Holl, and rewards or punishes them in accordance with their treatment of him. The opinion of some authorities is that the gipsies (Bohemians) who seemed to have spread over the entire Austrian dominions before 1300, seized upon this legend and invented such designs as seemed to fit in with it and used them upon their fortune-telling cards.

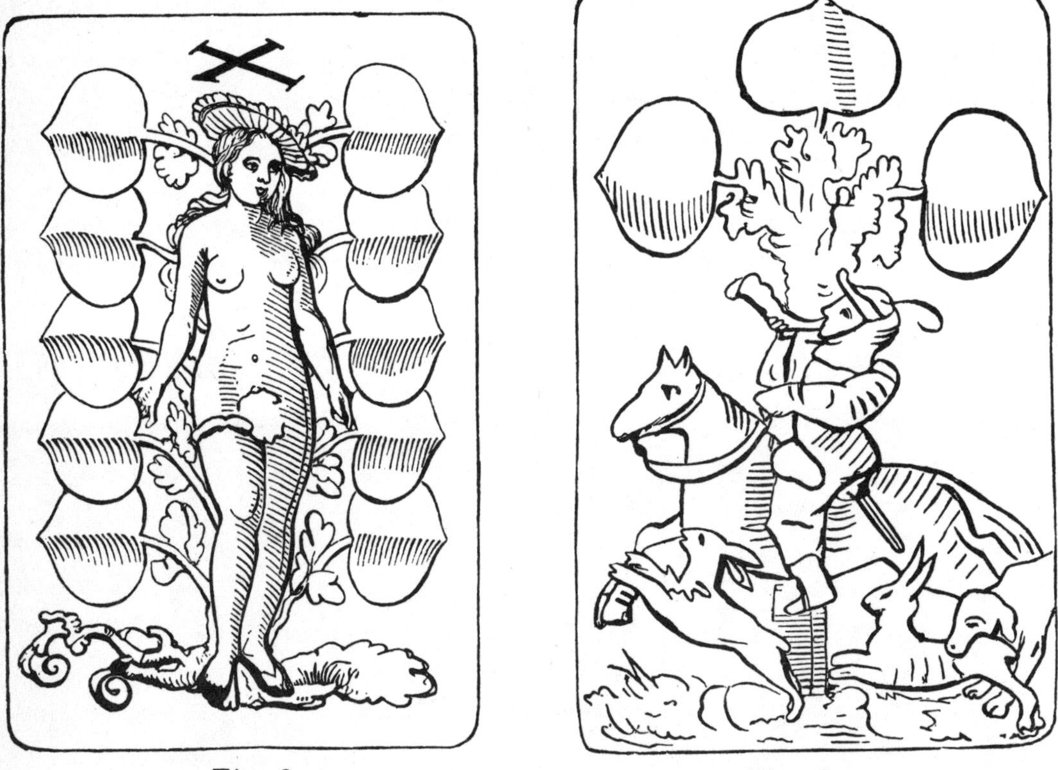

Fig. 80. Fig. 81.

There is also an old German pack, found behind the wainscoating of an ancient house in Nurnberg, the designs of which illustrate various incidents, which can be traced to the same Bohemian legend. Fig. 80 shows the ten of Leaves belonging to this pack. A nude woman is portrayed standing with five large leaves on either side of her and some smaller foliage at the back. On the three of the same suit a huntsman and his dogs are pursuing a hare and leaves of the same shape are in evidence. Fig. 81. It is interesting to note how the leaves gradually changed their shape as the years went by and fresh packs were made, and eventually became our modern Hearts. The stems were omitted, and the leaves were drawn perhaps slightly overlapping each other, until at last the suit sign developed into the one shown in Fig. 82, the three of Hearts.

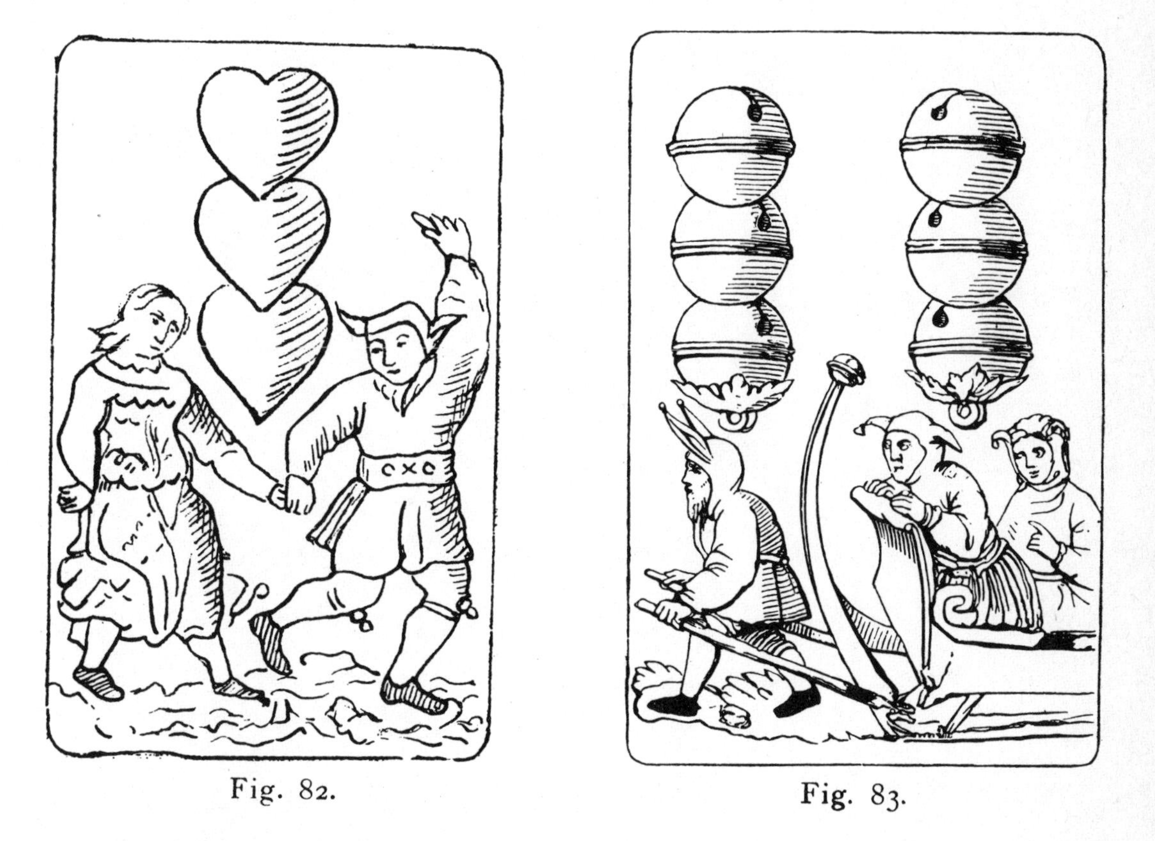

Fig. 82. Fig. 83.

The six of Bells (Fig. 83) which also belongs to this pack, introduces another character from the legend, the fool, with his bells, who sits in a sleigh with a lady by his side.

The other two suits in this pack are Acorns and Roses.

Israel van Mecken, (?) cir. 1470.

A rare pack of forty-seven German cards is in the British Museum. These are from a series of fifty-two cards, the suits of which are Batons, Cups, Swords and Pomegranates. The three of cups, the nine, ten, valet and king of pomegranates are missing. The designs are from copper-plate engravings and have been attributed to Israel van Mecken or to Martin Schoengauer (probably about 1470). The honour cards are King, Queen and Valet, and generally better designed and executed than any of the other cards.

Fig. 84. Fig 85.

Fig. 86. Fig. 87.

Here are particulars of a few of the cards from each suit :

SUIT OF SWORDS.

On the two is shown a kneeling hermit, asking alms of a lady.
On the three (Fig. 84), is a sow with five small pigs.
On the nine St. George is seen fighting with the Dragon.

SUIT OF CUPS.

On the ace is an ornamental fountain. Two men, each with three hawks, are standing on the brim and above are two cupids discharging their arrows. Page 8.

On the seven are seven cups, each of a different design.

On the Queen a lady in handsome dress is holding a cup in her right hand.

On the Valet, Fig. 87, a young gentleman very gaily dressed and with long curls, seated upon horseback, holding a cup.

SUIT OF POMEGRANATES (OR FRUIT).

On the Ace (Fig. 85), two children within the opened fruit are quarelling for the seeds. Above are five birds.

On the seven, two boys are fighting, while below is a Jester, or Fool.

The Queen holds a pomegranate in her hand and a naked child is emerging from a flower.

SUIT OF BATONS.

On the three a centaur is shown fighting two dragons. Fig. 86.

On the seven are birds, flowers, and some fine arabesque ornamentation.

On the King an aged man with a crown upon his head is seated on a throne holding a large stick or baton.

Whilst these are labelled "trappola cards," it should be noted that the game of trappola is played with a series of numerals, of which the 3, 4, 5 and 6 of each suit are omitted, but as this pack has all the low cards, they could not have been intended solely for the game of trappola, although the latter game could no doubt be played with them if the low cards mentioned were rejected.

The Valets are always represented on horseback, the Kings, holding the symbols of their suits, are seated on rich thrones, and the Queens are all wearing elegant draperies. The designs generally show groups of figures, often of a grotesque or humourous character. On the three of swords is a scroll bearing the words "*Ante...Motorum Meus.*" (see Fig. 84). On the ten of Cups are the letters C.B.F.S.A., and on the ten of Batons, J.N.R.Z.Q.

This rare series formerly belonged to Dr. Silberrad of Nurnberg, then to Count de Fries at Vienna, and eventually it was purchased by the British Museum. Breitkopf shows nine of these engravings in his work on the origin of playing cards. Chatto shows four, and Mr. Ottley, in his "Facsimiles of Scarce and Curious Engravings," London, 1826, has introduced the whole forty-seven pieces, with a short description of each.

Lucas Cranach (?), cir. 1515.

Like most of the other countries of Europe, Germany lays claim to the honour of having invented playing cards, and one writer (a Dominican Friar) says they were known in Germany at the beginning

Obermann of Acorns, Fig. 88.*

Obermann of Leaves, Fig. 89.*

of the 14th century. Another claims the honour from the fact that "Brieft" (meaning letters) is the name often given to cards in Germany, although "Karten" is an older name for them.*

The German cards of the 15th and 16th centuries are often very fanciful, and frequently contain (in addition to the pips and suit signs) illustrations showing groups of men and women, birds, animals, and flowers, and the Coat cards are especially interesting, although sometimes indecent.

* Chatto, 236 and 237.

Fig. 90, Untermann of Acorns.

Fig. 91, King of Hearts.

Fig. 92, Two of Bells.

Fig. 93, Six of Leaves.

In Fig. 88 we have the Obermann of Acorns (*Eicheln*), and in Fig. 89 the Obermann of Leaves (*Grun*), from a pack engraved about 1515. They are supposed to be the work of Lucas Cranach, a celebrated engraver on wood, and the figures are well drawn with great freedom, and full of spirit and possess a good deal of artistic merit, and are probably intended to illustrate members of the various trades and professions. On the Knave (or Obermann) of Hearts there is the itinerant barber, with his squirrel on his shoulder and carrying the various implements of his trade. Fig. 89 represents the scribe or letter writer.

Another German pack of 36 cards is represented on page 74. The four suits are Acorns (*Eicheln*), Bells (*Schellen*), Hearts (*Herzen*), and Leaves (*Grun*). The Court cards are King, Obermann, and Untermann, but no Queen. The numeral cards are the 2, 6, 7, 8, 9 and 10. The two of Leaves and Hearts bear heraldic shields and on the two of Acorns there are three shields and also a scroll with the wording "*Feine Schwerdter Karte,*" and on the eight of Hearts the maker's name "*Carl Heinrich Zolete in Liepzig.*" All the numeral cards have in addition to the suit marks, various illustrations as shown on two of Bells, Fig. 92, and six of Leaves, Fig. 93. The Unter of Acorns is shown on Fig. 90, the King of Hearts on Fig. 91. They are all finished in very brilliant colouring. Fig. 4, Frontispiece, shows the Unter of Acorns in facsimile.

Another pack, dated "*der* 18 *Oct.* 1813" contains only 24 cards, each suit having King, Obermann and Untermann, and 2, 9 and 10, making six of each suit of Acorns, Bells, Hearts and Leaves. The maker's name "*I. E. Backhofen,*" is on the two of Acorns, and the shape is somewhat unusual, each card being almost square.

Fig. 94.

Fig. 94. is a reduced copy of a card, the three of Bells, taken from an early 16th century pack (cir. 1510) in the Paris Library, some of which are illustrated by D'Ambly in his book "Les Cartes a Jouer."* It shows a very lively scene where two women are quarrelling, and the honours appear fairly equal. The designs are probably by Lucas Cranach, and shows the humorous spirit of the times.

* Page 94.

German Educational Pack.

Among the many nations who claim to have been the first to attempt the use of playing cards as a means of instruction, the Germans, according to M. la Croix, seem to stand out as the most probable originators of this idea.

In order to aid pupils in their studies there were issued cards whereon were printed illustrations of and instruction in music, heraldry, astronomy, arithmetic, poetry, stories of ancient history, &c., and pupils were supposed to become interested in the various branches of learning while fondly imagining they were enjoying a game. Whether or not the desired result was attained is not certain.

Fig. 95.

The eight of Bells, Fig. 95, is from an old German pack said to have been used by Dr. Thomas Murner* for educational purposes, and we wonder what the meaning can be of the various signs and symbols.

* See page 208.

His satanic Majesty is seen working at a potter's wheel (?) while the young gentleman with his hands tied together appears to be pleading for his release. At the top of the card the Sun and the Moon would seem to be trying to eclipse each other. This pack dates from about 1507, and it is the earliest instance known of playing cards being used as a means of education. The Doctor is said to have made each card an aid to memory.

Fig. 96.

Fig. 97.

In another 16th century pack also believed to have been used by him the following sixteen signs are used as suit signs :—

Pigeons	Cats	Crayfish	Scorpions
Acorns	Turbans	Suns	Crescents
Grasshoppers	Hearts	Stars	Coats of Arms
Fish	Crowns	Serpents	Bells

Fig. 96, the four of Scorpions, shows a woman, seated upon a goat, which has in its mouth a pair of compasses. The woman holds an hour glass in her left hand, and in her right hand appears to be an equinoctial circle (?). Four scorpions, a variety of articles, and the numerals 2, 6, 7 and 4 are scattered over the card.

On the eight of Fishes (Fig. 97) we have two naked children who appear to be quarrelling. One holds an hour-glass and the other a target with four darts. A large cock carries a cross and rosary in its claw. The eight of fishes, together with a pot out of which flames are issuing, and over thirty letters and numerals are also upon this card.

On the two of Acorns, a lady carrying a long spear, is seated upon a horse. Five very large feathers are in her head-dress, and a shield is upon her right shoulder. At the bottom of the card are three dogs tied together.

All the cards have letters and numerals upon them, sometimes combined, as in Fig. 97, but it is not very clear how they could have helped Dr. Murner's pupils in their studies.

Jost Ammon, cir. 1570.

Fig. 98.

Jost Ammon, cir. 1570.

One of the most interesting packs of cards is one designed and beautifully engraved on wood by Jost Ammon * about 1570. It was no doubt intended to inculcate the advantages of Industry and Learning over Idleness and Drunkenness. The designs used on this pack were also published in a small volume of sixty-four leaves, which contained fifty-two engravings accompanied by German and Latin verse.† There is no queen among them, and the Court cards are Kings, Superior and Inferior Officers. The four suits are *Books, Printers' Inking Balls, Glass or Earthenware Wine Vases* and *Metal Drinking Cups*. Generally the subject on each card is treated in a humorous manner, but the drawings are full of life and very carefully executed. Artizans at their work, domestic scenes, music and dancing, are all represented.

The suit of Books is emblematical of learning, and on Fig. 99 we have the two of that suit, which shows us in a very spirited print the Bookbinder at his work. Fig. 98, shows the four and five of Books.

Fig. 99.

Fig. 100.

* Page 313. † Singer, 181.

The three of Books (Fig. 100) illustrates the old story of the wolf turned schoolmaster. He is seen pointing out the letters of the alphabet to three geese, one of whom has his school bag hanging on its neck.

On the five of Books a drunken pedlar has set down his basket of horn books which an ape is busily emptying, while two other apes are tormenting the pedlar as he lies on the ground, Fig. 98. The verses accompanying this print express the advantages of sobriety. The Ace of Books is a large open book surrounded by foliage.

The two of Printers' Inking Balls (Fig. 101) shows a printer working at an old standing press, which he is just pulling over to take an impression, while his assistant stands with the two inking balls waiting to ink up the forme again ready for another impression. The three of this suit (*Fig.* 102) is singularly appropriate to the subject of this book, as it shows a lady and gentleman seated at a table on which is a lighted candle and a pack of cards. A dog is seated by the side of the lady, who holds a goblet in her right hand and a card in her left, and judging by the air of quiet assurance with which she is showing the latter to the gentleman, it seems certain that she holds a card which she knows he cannot beat. Fig. 98, shows the four and five of Printers' Inking Balls.

Fig. 101.

Fig. 102.

The two of Vases, Fig. 103, shows two peasants who are enjo ing themselves in a lively dance. The three of the same suit, Fig. 104, depicts a man and woman seated at dinner, and while the woman is drinking from a very large cup a dog drags a chicken from the dish. The man, who is holding a bag of money in his hand, appears to be in a drunken stupor. Fig. 98, shows the four and five of Vases.

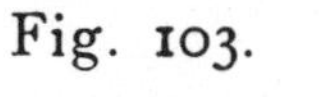

Fig. 103.

Fig. 104.

The Suit of Wine Cups illustrates the folly of taking too much wine, and on the Ace we see a man who has indulged too freely with the result that he is very sick. On the four are a drunken couple. The husband is beating his wife, who holds him by his hair to prevent herself falling to the ground. Fig. 98, shows the four and five of Wine Cups.

Some of the suits extol the delights of music and singing.

Illustrations of the suit of Drinking Cups are shown on page 82, where on the two, Fig. 105, is a well drawn group of musicians. On the three, Fig. 106, is a gentleman on horseback who appears to be taking leave of his weeping lady love. Fig. 98, shows the four and five of Drinking Cups.

Singer* speaking of the designer of this pack (Jost Ammon), says, "The spirit of the designs in his Book of Trades, and on these cards, is, perhaps, not exceeded by any woodcuts of the same period when numbers of excellent artists flourished and the quantity of engravings executed, both on wood and on copper, is almost beyond belief."

Fig. 105.

Fig. 106.

* Singer, page 198.

Royal Household Servants, 15th century.

A most interesting pack of German cards (described by Henry Rene d'Allemagne*) was published in the 15th century, and illustrates the Officers, Servants and various other dependants attached to a Royal household.

The four suits are heraldic, and may be emblazoned thus -:—
" *Azure, three fleurs-de-lys, or.*" (France). Figs. 107 and 111.
"*Barry of eight, azure and gules.*" (Hungary). Fig. 109.
" *A lion rampant, double queld crowned or.*" (Bohemia). Fig. 110.
" *An eagle displayed.*" (Holy Empire.) Figs. 108 and 112.

Fig. 107.

* Cartes a jouer, Rene d'Allemagne, page 386.

The tens, Fig. 108 to 111 (reduced about half size) show the four Masters of the Court.

Nines show the four Marshals in armour on horseback.

Eights show Chaplain, Physician, Chancellor and Mistress of the Court.

Fig. 108.

Fig. 109.

Fig. 110.

Fig. 111.

Sevens are the Cupbearer, Fig. 107, the Chamberlain, the Chief Cook and the Grand Master of the Kitchen, Fig. 112.

Sixes are the four Ladies in Waiting.

Fives are the Butler, Falconer, Huntsman and Cook.

Fours are the Barber, Riding Master and two Trumpeters.

Threes are the Groom, Fisherman, Tailor, Herald.

Twos are Footman, Messenger, Kitchen Maid, Scullion.

Aces are two male and two female Clowns.

Fig. 112.

As will be seen by the two cards, Figs. 107 and 112 each officer or servant is doing something connected with his or her particular calling.

Fig. 113.

Fig. 114.

Fig. 115.

Fig. 116.

German Luxury Cards.

A pack, published at Frankfort, at the end of the 19th century, and termed "*Luxus Spielkarten*," has upon the forty numeral cards a series of very clever illustrations by Hausmann. The four suits have designs which represent scenes connected with the history of the four great continents, and particulars of each design are given in a leaflet which was issued in English and German to accompany the pack.

SPADES FOR AFRICA.

The King of Spades, Fig. 113,* is represented by *the Sultan*. The Queen is his *Sultana,* and the Knave *a Janizay*. The ten, termed "*the Guardian of the Treasure*," shows a crocodile keeping watch over a large key. The eight is called "*the Happy Lover*," and the three "*the Pensive Favourite.*"

HEARTS FOR ASIA.

Here the King of Hearts is repesented by "*The Great Mogul*," The Queen by a "*Hindoo Princess*," and the Knave by a "*Hindoo Warrior.*" The design on the three of hearts, Fig. 114., shows the Indian custom of "*Suttee*," and is explained thus "*Widow ascending the funeral pile.*" The five shows two Nabobs playing at chess.

DIAMONDS FOR EUROPE.

Here the King is "*The Emperor*," and the Queen, "*The Empress*," while the Knave is "*The Lance Bearer.*" On the nine is a *Hunting Scene,* and on the three is "*The Art of Printing*," showing Caxton, standing by an old-fashioned printing press, examining some of his work. Fig. 116.

CLUBS FOR AMERICA.

Although numeral cards of this Suit illustrate American scenes, the Coat cards are Spanish, the King being "*King Ferdinand*," with "*Queen Isabella*," and the Knave is "*A Spanish Ambassador.*" The three of Clubs, Fig. 115, illustrates "*Columbus landing in the New World.*"

The Ace of the suit of Hearts bears an Indian Prince on an Elephant; that of Diamonds, Justice with the scales and sword; Spades has an Egyptian scene; Clubs, a fully rigged sailing vessel. The Court cards are all highly coloured, but the designs on the numeral cards are printed very lightly in a pale grey tone.

* Also in colours, see frontispiece.

Erhardt Schoen, (?) cir. 1460.

The date of the adoption by the Germans of the suits of SCHELLEN (Bells), HERZEN (Hearts), GRUN (Green Leaves), and EICHELN (Acorns), is not known, but early in the fifteenth century we find representations of various devices used, such as birds, plants, human figures, various animals, fruit and flowers, and much skill and taste is often displayed in the designs. A card from one of these packs, the six of Roses Fig. 117, shows four peasants dancing to the sound of a bagpipe. Two of the dancers appear to be kissing as well as dancing. In Fig. 118, the five of Leaves, another kissing scene is shown, but the lady, while submitting to the caresses of an elderly man, is giving her hand to a younger swain. On the Valet of Grapes the monogram E.S.† is engraved. The five of Pomegranates* shows a man playing upon a flageolet and a woman performing upon a mandolin. Both are apparently accompanying a girl who is singing. The four suits are Leaves, Roses, Pomegranates and Grapes.‡

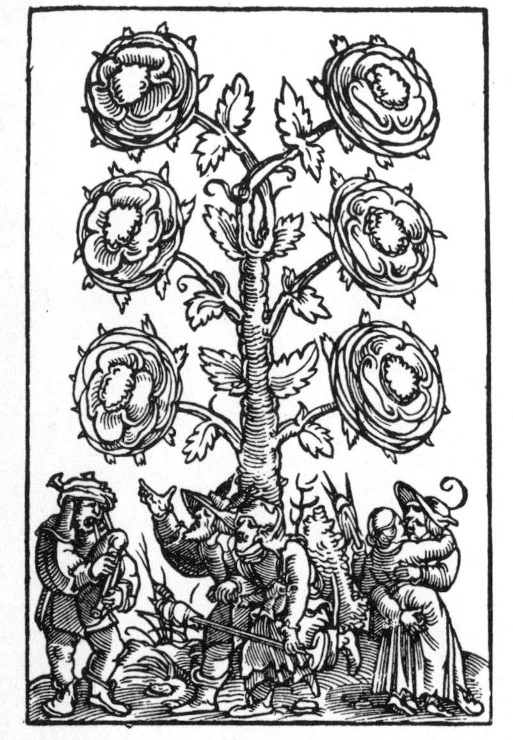

Fig. 117.

Fig. 118.

† Erhardt Schoen.

* Fig. 85

‡ Singer, pages 42-43.

Transformation, cir. 1806.

A Pack consisting of fifty two cards with the usual suit signs, was issued cir. 1806 in Tubingen. On the Ace of Clubs (which partly forms the body of a large beetle) are the words " *A Tubinge chez, T. G. Cotta, Libraire*," and the pack is probably the first of a series which appeared in Germany known as " Almanack " cards. These were published by T. G. Cotta annually for some years. Fig. 119 shows the seven of Spades cleverly designed to form the hoods of seven monks.

Fig. 119.

The two and three of clubs and the four of Diamonds are almost exactly the same as the pack designed by "Olivatte" Figs. 223 to 227, which are evidently copied from this pack which appeared some 22 years previously. Chatto says the Coat cards represent the principal characters in Schiller's *Joan of Arc*. The King of Hearts represents *Charles VII*; the Queen, *Isabella of Bavaria*; the Knave *La Hire*. The Queen of Clubs is "*Joan of Arc*." The King of Spades " *Rene of Anjou*," and the Queen " *Louise, sister of Joan of Arc*."

Many of the designs are clever, and better finished than the pack described on page 152.

Oval Cards, Modern.

Fig. 234 shows the Dame of Spades from a double-ended pack, of 32 oval cards printed at Dresden, bearing French names on the Court cards. Each suit consists of Roi, Dame, and Valet, with the numerals ace, seven, eight, nine, and ten, making eight cards in each suit. They have the suit marks all round the edge, and on the pip cards (seven to ten) the value is marked on each pip in a white Roman figure. The Coat cards represent Knowledge, War, Peace and Industry.

On Hearts. (*Knowledge*).

The Roi holds a globe.
The Dame is writing on a scroll.
The Valet is writing in a book.

On Spades. (*War*).

The Roi is holding a sword.
The Dame, Fig. 227, holds a long spear.
The Valet holds a large double-handed sword.

On Clubs. (*Peace*).

The Roi is a stocky yeoman.
The Dame is a maiden with two doves.
The Valet a labourer with his dog.

On Diamonds (*Industry*).

The Roi is a merchant with a money-bag.
The Dame is a lady with needlework.
The Valet is a man with a pair of scales and a yard measure.

The ace of hearts has the duty stamp upon it, e.g., the German eagle and the wording "Deutsches Reich, No. 59 Dreissig G.F."; and on the Valet of Spades there is the maker's name, A. Trivetmeyer, Leipzig.

17th Century.

Four cards from another 17th century pack illustrate on the four of Acorns Fig. 120 a hunting scene; on the six of Hearts Fig. 121, a lady and gentleman arm in arm; on the three of Leaves Fig. 123, a drummer vigorously applying his sticks, while Fig. 122 is the Obermann of Leaves. These are much smaller than usual.

Fig. 120.

Fig. 121.

Fig. 122.

Chatto 239.

Fig. 132.

Tarot Pack (Mayer) cir. 1730.

Here are two cards from an old Tarot pack published by JOANNES PELAGIUS MAYER, in Constance, about 1730. Fig. 124 represents the TWO OF CUPS and Fig. 125 TWO OF MONEY.

The pack is made up of the 16 Coat cards and 40 numerals, to which are added the 22 Atout cards, making 78 in all. The suit signs are Cups for Faith, Money for Charity, Swords for Justice, and Clubs for Fortitude.

The cards are rather larger than usual, measuring $4\frac{1}{2}$ in. by $2\frac{1}{2}$ in. They are carelessly drawn and are badly coloured by means of stencils.

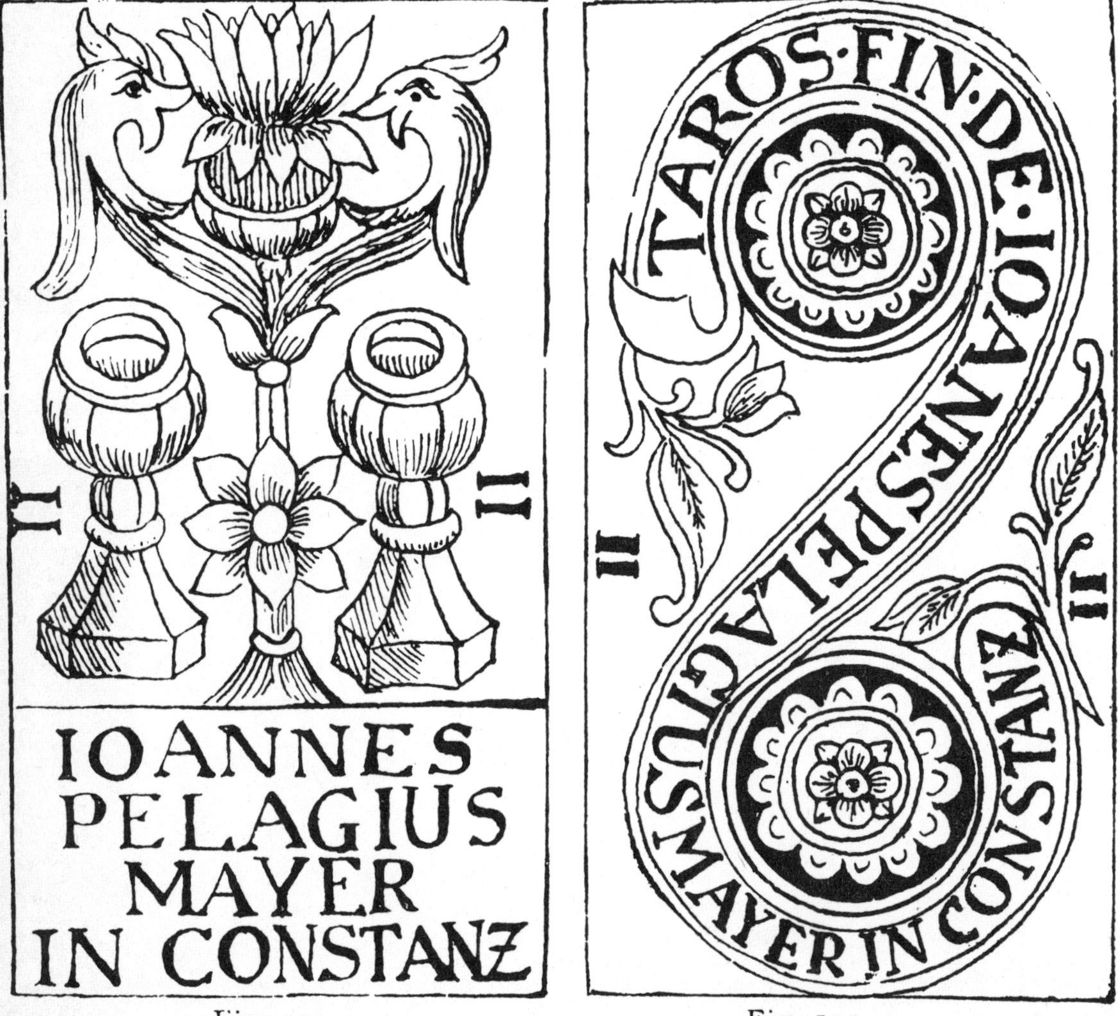

Fig. 124. Fig. 125.

Astronomical, cir. 1656.

These four cards are from an Astronomical pack. The suit marks are at the top of the cards, while below are illustrations and particulars of the various constellations. These were no doubt intended for use in teaching Astronomy.

The first . . Three of leaves with Constellation showing Ursa Major, the Great Bear.
The second . King of Acorns with Capricornus, the Goat.
The third . Six of Bells, with (?) Leo, the Lion.
The fourth . Four of Hearts with (?) Sagittarius, the Archer.

Made by Endter of Nurnberg. Date 1656.

Astronomical, 1656. **Fig. 126.**

Fig. 127. Fig. 128.

The four cards Fig. 127, are very early German Atouts by Hans Sebald Beham about 1520–40.

The four shown on Fig. 128, are 17th century German. They are the 4 of Hearts (or Leaves), the King of Acorns, the Fou of Atouts and the Knave of Swords.

Pencil Drawn Pack, cir. 1440.

A pack of playing cards, dating from about 1440, is illustrated by forty-nine photographs and explanatory notes in "*Studies in the History of German Art.*" The originals are pencil drawings, and the four suits are quite unique as they are represented by

ENTEN	—	Ducks	FALKEN	—	Falcons
HUNDE	—	Hounds or Dogs	HIRSCHE	—	Stags

The numeral cards one to nine, have upon them the same number of Ducks, Dogs, Falcons and Stags which correspond to the value of the card, but the tens have only one of the suit signs, which in each case is displayed upon a banner, as seen in Fig. 129 which shows THE HIRSCH BANNER (Ten of Stags). The Coat cards have the same three names generally found on old German playing-cards, viz.:—King, Ober and Unter (Superior and Inferior Officers).

The ENTEN-KONIG (King of Ducks) in very elaborate dress, is on horse-back. He holds a banner in his right hand, and a single duck is shown on the ground near the horse's feet, Fig. 130.

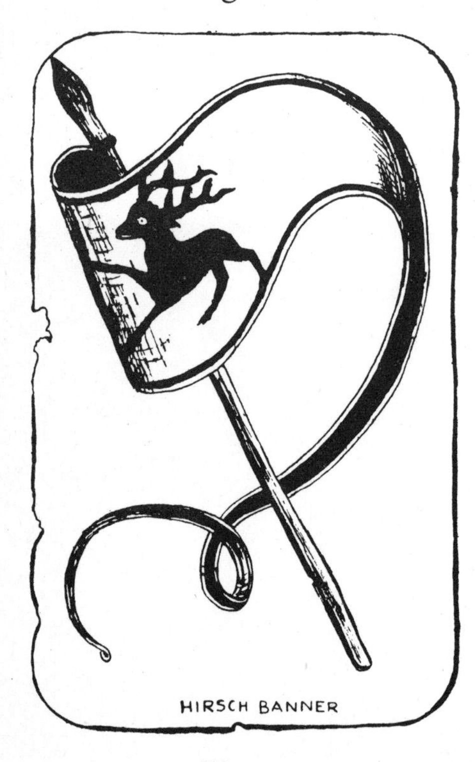

Fig. 129.

Fig. 130.

The ENTEN OBER is a young man who is holding a duck aloft by the neck.

The ENTEN-UNTER is a lad who is feeding a duck.

All the three Coat cards on the suit of Hunde (Dogs) are ladies in long flowing dresses.

The King of Dogs, HUNDE-KONIGIN, is shown as a lady with a small dog near her right hand.

The HUNDE-OBERHOFDAME shown in Fig. 132 is a tall lady, who is caressing a dog.

The HUNDE-UNTERHOFDAME is also a full length figure of a lady, with a very large dog crouching at her side.

The King on the suit of Falcons, (FALKEN-KONIG) is shown holding a banner and seated upon a white horse covered with very elaborate harness, and on the ground a large falcon is seen.

The FALKEN OBER is a young man who has a falcon perched upon his left wrist.

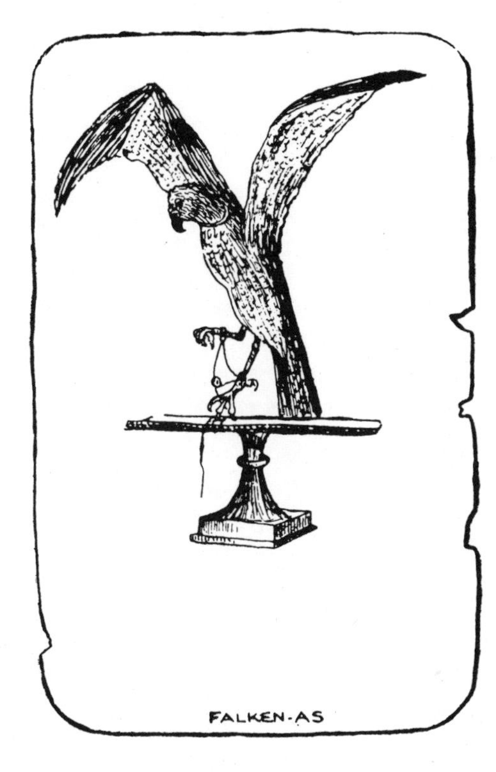

Fig. 131.

Fig. 132.

The FALKEN-UNTER is missing.

The Ace of Falcons FALKEN-AS Fig. 131, shows a single falcon, with wings outspread, fastened by its leg to an ornamental stand.

The Coat cards on the suit of Stags are also three ladies.

The King of Stags, HIRSCH-KONIGIN, is shown as a lady seated upon a couch, and fondling a young stag.

The HIRSCH-OBERHOFDAME is an older lady in a very high-waisted dress, holding the forefoot of a stag which is standing on its hind legs.

The HIRSCH-UNTERHOFDAME shows a lady with a large stag crouching at her side.

NOTE:—The three superior cards, King, Obermann, and Untermann, on the suits of Dogs and Stags are women, but on the suits of Falcons and Ducks they are men.

These cards are from Max Geisberg's "*Collection of Playing Cards*" and are in the Royal State Collection of Antiquities in Stuttgart.

Fig. 133.

Caliographic Pack, cir. 1770.

A pack published in Nurnberg, Germany, cir. 1770, consists of ingenious pen drawings illustrating different characters, and with letters of the alphabet scattered over the cards. Fig. 133, shows the Nine of Hearts, and seems to represent, according to the wording, a Scotch Highlander with his kilt, bagpipes, sword and spear. The drawing of the figure is one continuous line, and commencing at the bottom of the sword a single line can be traced over the whole of the figure, finishing close to where it commences.

FRENCH CARDS.
Tarot Pack, cir. 1500.

D'Ambly* illustrates six cards which he says belong to a pack manufactured in Paris about 1500. They are well engraved and the figures represented are full of life. They are part of a Tarot pack, and are much larger than present-day cards, and a bold chequered border runs all round the edge of each card. At the top are two animals holding a small scroll upon which is the number or initials of the card.

The Ace of Money (*Ar de Deniers*) Fig. 134, shows a lion rampant holding a large banner upon which is a circle with three fleur de lis, and the letters A. D. at top.

Fig. 134.

* Les Cartes a Jouer by P. Boiteau D' Ambly, page 8.

THE QUEEN OF SWORDS (*Royne d'Espee*) Fig. 135, shows a finely built woman, who holds a sword in her left hand, as if just about to strike.

THE CHEVALIER OF BATONS (*Chevalier de Baston*) Fig. 36 is a man on horse-back holding a large club.

This pack probably consisted of 40 Numeral Cards, 16 Coat Cards and 22 Atouts = 78.

Fig. 135. Fig. 136.

The three just described are from the pack of 56 cards the suits of which are Money, Cups, Swords and Batons. There are two others taken from the Atouts, one, THE EMPEROR (*Lanperevt*) Fig. 138 shows a man crowned and in full plate armour, over which is a large cloak. He grasps a massive sword in his left hand, and represents Atout No. IIII*. The other, THE WORLD (*Le Monde*) Fig. 137 shows a nude woman standing upon a globe, on which are various mystical signs. She holds a large banner in her right hand, and below are a number of heads representing the four winds. This is Atout No. XXI.‡

Fig. 137. Fig. 138.

* Fig. 14. ‡ Fig. 35.

Animals & Birds, cir. 1600.

Three cards are illustrated from a French pack in which the suits are Peacocks, Lions, Parrots and Monkeys. The Coat cards are cleverly drawn, showing figures full of life. The numeral cards have the number of birds or animals from one to ten, worked into either a conventional or a fancy design, as shown in Fig. 139, which represents the eight of lions. Fig. 140 shows the four of peacocks, and Fig. 141 the four of monkeys. At the top of each card the value is printed in Roman figures.

On the Ace of Peacocks the word GRVEN with a monogram V.S. is engraved, and on the two of Monkeys are the letters S.P.Q.R.

The pack dates from about 1600.

Fig. 139.

IIII

Fig. 140.

Fig. 141.

Cards by Jean Des-Marets, cir. 1644.

During the reign of Louis XIV a number of packs of cards were published by a French Academician, Jean Des-Marets (or Desmarests). It is said that Cardinal Mazarin (himself a great card player), suggested to him to prepare a series of games with cards, with the idea of imparting instruction to the young King. Four series were produced, and letter-patent (dated 1644) was granted to Des-Marets, giving him certain monopolies connected with cards, and forbidding the sale by anyone, other than his own publishers, under a penalty of 3000 livres.

One series entitled "LE JEU DES FABLES" (*The Game of Fables*) has upon each card a clever little engraving representing some of the heroes, demi-gods, &c., of antiquity and classical history, and under this a short explanation with the suit mark and card value.

The ACE OF CLUBS, Fig. 142, shows "ARION,"* (a celebrated lyric poet and musician) seated upon a dolphin and playing the Cithara an instrument like a violin.

Fig. 142.

Fig. 143.

* P. B D' Ambly, page 133.

The historical characters represented on the Coat cards are :—

	KINGS.	QUEENS.	VALETS.
SPADES	Saturn.	Venus.	Apollon.
HEARTS	Jupiter.	Juno.	Mars.
CLUBS	Neptune.	Pallas.	Mercury.
DIAMONDS	Pluton.	Diane.	Bacchus.

Another series, "LE JEU DES ROIS," consists of illustrations of various French kings from Pharamond (A.D. 418) down to Louis XIV, with short biographies of their reigns.

The Eight of Spades, Fig. 143 gives particulars of Henry the Second, who died of a wound received at a tournament, A.D. 1547.

In the third series "LE JEU DE LA GEOGRAPHIE" the four suits represent the four great continents, each having thirteen different designs, made up as follows :—

SPADES. Asia. HEARTS. Europe.
DIAMONDS. Africa. CLUBS. America.

Fig. 144.

Fig. 145.

The game of Renowned Queens.

The fourth series "LE JEU DES REYNES RENOMMEES" shows on each card an illustration of one of the queens of history. There are thirteen divisions of four, each classified under the following card values :—

Kings—4 Saintly Women.	Sevens—4 Good Women.
Queens—4 Celebrated.	Sixes—4 Licentious.
Valets—4 Brave.	Fives—4 Courageous.
Tens—4 Pious.	Fours—4 Clever.
Nines—4 Wise.	Threes—4 Capricious.
Eights—4 Cruel.	Twos—4 Unfortunate.

Aces—4 Happy Women.

Queen Elizabeth is placed among the four Clever Women, and Mary Stuart among the four unfortunate Women. The Queen of Sheba, Fig. 144, on the Nine of Hearts, is placed among the four "Wise, Women. The four Kings (Women) *Anne d'Austriche, Blanche de Castille, Bandour, Clotilde,* are shown in Chariots, and the four Queens, *Zenobie, Tomyris, Semiramis, Didon* are on horses.

The engravings are attributed to the Florentine artist-engraver Stefano de la Bella.

Hand Painted Pack, cir. 1490.

Three cards from a beautifully finished hand-drawn and painted pack, date from the end of the XV century, and show the costume as worn in France during the reign of Charles VII.*

The Queen of Spades, Fig. 146, is shown with the steeple head-dress and long veil. The Knave of Hearts, Fig. 147, has a fine ermine mantle and holds in his right hand a lighted torch. The Knave of Clubs, Fig. 148, holds a large spear and his doublet is most elaborately embroidered. The King of Hearts holds a sword. The King of Spades a large dart, and the Kings of Diamonds and Clubs hold scrolls.

* Cartes a jouer, Rene D' Allemagne.

Hand Painted, cir. 1490.

Fig. 146. Fig. 147. Fig. 148.

Fig. 149.

Fig. 150.

Heraldic, cir. 1692.

Heraldry has often been used on playing cards and some very fine examples of engraving were executed during the latter half of the 17th and beginning of the 18th centuries, illustrating the coats of arms of Royalty and of the Nobility, Cardinals and high dignitaries of most of the European countries.

An Heraldic Pack of 52 cards, using (instead of the ordinary pips) the arms of the Nobility of France, Germany, Italy, Spain and Portugal, was published in the reign of Louis XIV at Lyons by Thomas Almaury, about 1692.

They are printed from engraved copper plates and are well designed and beautifully finished as may be seen in Figs. 149 and 150, where the Queen of Lions and the Three of Roses are shown.

The Coat cards are King, Queen and Chevalier, and the suit signs are :—

FLEUR DE LYS......France.	LIONS...... Spain and Portugal
ROSES...............Italy.	EAGLES ..... Germanic States.

The King of Fleur de Lys (France) represents Louis XIV with his motto "*Nec pluribus impar.*" The queen is Maria Therese, the Ace carries the arms of France, and the rest of the series have upon them the arms of the Chancelliers, Chevaliers du St. Esprit, Gentilshommes de la Chambre, Comtes de Lyon, and others.

In the suit of Roses (Italy) the King and Queen are the Duke and Duchess of Savoy (the Duchess was the daughter of Charles I of England). The Chevalier is the Grand-Master of Malta, and the other cards have the arms of Barons, Cardinals, Doges, and Dukes, engraved upon them. Fig. 150 shows the three of Roses (Nobles Lvqvois). In the Suit of Eagles (Germanic States) the King and Queen are the Emperor and Empress of Austria. The Emperor is shown seated upon his throne holding the imperial orb, and with a large eagle at his side. The Chevalier is the Master of the Teutonic Order and is holding a staff surmounted by an eagle and bearing the letters S.P.Q.R. On the six are engraved the six banners of Flanders, and on the ten the arms of the Princes of the Empire.

In the suit of Lions (Spain and Portugal) we have the King of Spain, with a large lion at his side. The Queen of Spain Fig. 149 is standing beside a table on which a lion is shown holding two shields bearing the arms of Castile and Spain. The Ace bears the arms of

Portugal, and on the other cards we have the arms of Barons, Nobles, and Dukes, and the following list will illustrate how, as the value of the card increases, so a higher order of society is represented.

Two	Seignvrs.	Eight	Comtes.
Three	Villes.	Nine	Marqvis.
Four	Prelates.	Ten	Dvcs.
Five	Chevaliers.	Chevalier.	
Six	Barons.	Reine Fig. 149.	
Seven	Nobles.	Roy	

Jehan Bourlion, cir. 1620.

A pack published about 1620 at Grenoble by Jehan Bourlion, is one of a series in which the Coat cards bear portraits of the reigning Kings, Queens, and Princes. The King of Spades, Fig. 151, probably represents LOUIS XIII and the Queen, Fig. 152, may be intended for MARY DE MEDICIS, who governed France during the minority of Louis. Fig. 153 is no doubt a portrait of the DAUPHIN as Knave or Prince.*

Fig. 151. Fig. 152. Fig. 153.

* Cartes a Jouer, Rene D' Allemagne.

Heraldic, M. de Brainville, cir. 1660.

A pack of Heraldic Cards was invented about 1660 by a M. de Brainville at Lyons, in which the Aces and Knaves (les As et Valets) were represented by the arms of certain princes and nobles. As this was evidently a breach of etiquette and a slur upon the heraldic nobility, the plates were seized by the magistrates. However, as it appeared that Mons. de Brainville had given offence through inadvertence, the plates were restored to him on condition that he altered the odious names of "As" and "Valets" to "Princes", and "Chevaliers."

Another pack, on the same lines as the above, was published about 1670, the four suits being distinguished respectively by the armorial bearings of the kingdoms, provinces and great dignitaries of Italy, France, Spain, and the North. The honours, of course, contain the most exalted names. The Kings are marked R, the Queens (represented by men) D, the Valets P, and the Aces C.

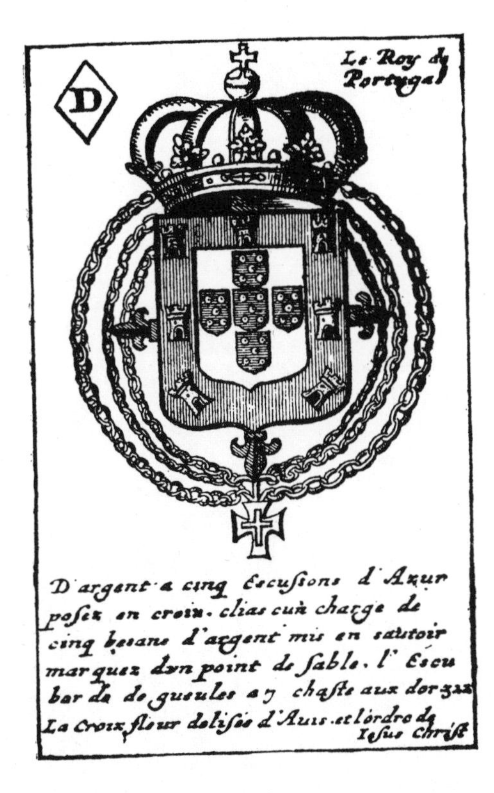

Fig. 154. Queen of Diamonds.

Fig. 155.

Fig. 156.

Fig. 157.

Fig. 158. Ten of Spades.

Fig. 159.

The arms on the honours cards are :—

CLUBS.

King	.	Le Pope. Alexander VII, *Fabio Chigi.*
Queen	.	Naples. (King of Naples).
Prince	.	S.A.R. de Savoy. (Duke of Savoy).
Ace	.	Les Republiques. (Venise, Geneo, Luques).

HEARTS.

King	.	The Roy de France. (King of France).
Queen	.	Fils de France. (Son of France).
Prince	.	Princes du Sang. (Prince of the Blood).
Ace	.	Ducs et Pairs Ecclesiastiques. (Ecclesiastical Peers).

DIAMONDS.

King	.	Le Roy de'Espagne. (King of Spain).
Queen	.	The Roy de Portugal. (King of Portugal). Fig. 154.
Prince	.	Castille et Leon. (Castile and Leon).
Ace	.	Aragon. (Arragon).

SPADES.

King	.	L'Empereur. (Emperor of Austria). Fig. 155.
Queen	.	Le Roy de Hongrie et de Boheme etc. Fig. 156. (Hungary and Bohemia).
Prince	.	Le Roy de la Grand Bretagne. (King of Great Britain). Fig. 157.
Ace	.	Le Roy de Polagne. (King of Poland).

The ten of Spades shows arms of the King of Sweden, Fig. 158

Although the King of Great Britain is shown as the Prince (or Knave) of Spades, a similar pack engraved later in England altered the suits so that Hearts and Spades changed places and the King of Hearts (King of France), became the King of Spades and the Prince of Spades (King of Graet Britain) became the King of Hearts. The Emperor of Germany became the Queen, and Bohemia and Hungary became the Prince, with Poland as the Ace.

The three of Spades, Fig. 159, shows the arms of the seventeen provinces of the Lower Countries.

Vincent Goyraud, (?) cir. 1600.

A pack published at the end of the 16th century, bears the initials V.G. (probably Vincent Goyraud). These show upon the Coat cards the costume of the time of Henry IV* of Bourbon, King of Navarre (1589-1610).

The Kings are named Clovice, Solomon, Constantine and Augustus. The Queens are Dido† Clotilda, Penthesilia‡ and Elizabeth, who is shown in Fig. 160. She is crowned and holds in one hand a fan, and in the other a flower. She is wearing a deep collar and the straight and formal stomacher gives her a long and very small waist, which is exaggerated by an immense skirt open in front to show the embroidered petticoat. This is distended by means of the farthingale, the ancestor of the 19th century crinoline. The Coat cards of this period generally bear the names of mythological or celebrated characters, such as Jupiter, Bacchus, Crœsus, Priapus§, Juno, Ceres¶, Flora, Diana, Mercury, Sylvanus, Æsculapius** Actæon, &c.

Fig. 160.
From D'Ambly, page 111.

* Murdered by Francis Ravaillac.

† The founder of Carthage.

‡ Daughter of Mars. Queen of the Amazons.

§ Son of Bacchus.

¶ The Goddess of the Earth.

** The God of the Medical Art.

Circular Cards, Telman von Wesel.

In the Paris collection of playing cards there is a complete pack of fifty-two circular cards, $2\frac{3}{4}$ inches in diameter, the suits of which are hares (*lievre*), pinks (*d'œillet*), columbines, (*d'ancolie*), and parrots (*perroquet*), enclosed within a border of three lines, on which the letters T. W. are printed. These are generally supposed to be the initials of Telman von Wesel. The value of the pip cards is given twice, at the bottom in Roman figures and at the top in Arabic figures. There are no tens in the pack, but as there are four Court Cards, King, Queen, Over and Under Valets, the pack of fifty-two cards is completed.

On the Ace of Parrots Fig. 161, under a waving ribbon, a single bird is shown seated on a tree growing at the top of a small hill, and the wording on the scroll runs "*Quidquid, fasimus, venit ex alto.*"

Fig. 161. Fig. 162.

The four and five of Parrots have upon them four and five birds in various positions. Figs. 163 and 164. On the Ace of Hares, Fig. 165 a single hare is sitting upright under a ribbon upon which are the following words, "*Ave, mi drint me vin dærom, mot ic en lepus sin,*" which Chatto translates thus :—

"Me o'er fields men keen pursue, therefore I am the hare you view."

On the Ace of Columbines, and also on the Ace of Pinks are long ribbons, with Latin inscriptions, waving around a single flower of the respective suit.

The court cards show the Kings and Queens in costly robes seated on horses or mules covered with elaborate drapery. The Valets, superior and inferior, are shown running, shooting, or employed in various pursuits. The inferior Valet of Parrots has just discharged an arrow from a bow and the bird has caught it in its beak. The superior Valet of Hares, who is in Oriental costume, is carrying a hare head downwards in his right hand, and has a long lance resting on his left shoulder. In Fig. 162 the inferior Valet of Hares has a long spear and the Hare seems to be jumping towards him. The superior Valet of Pinks shows a man running at full speed, holding his sword to his side with his left hand, and carrying a large battle-axe over his right shoulder.

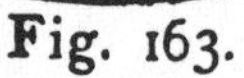

Fig. 163.

Fig. 164.

Fig. 165.

Fig. 166.

The Queen of Hares is wearing a coronet and her robe is spotted with fleur-de-lys. A cross projects from the head of her horse, which is most richly caparisoned. A hare is shown seated on a bank level with the lady.

The King of Columbines Fig. 166, is an old man on horseback, holding a sceptre and wearing a long cloak reaching almost to the ground.

M. Jacques, cir. 1475.

A pack designed by M. Jacques about 1475 has some very curious-looking figures on all the coat cards

Fig. 167 shows the King, who is wearing a large crown, and has a purse or bag hanging from his waist. The QUEEN, Fig. 168, has a veil hanging from the back of her crown and holds a small flower in her right hand. Her dress is embroidered and trimmed with ermine.

The VALET, Fig. 169, holds a large dart. His feet rest upon a scroll upon which the makers name "I.A.Q.U.E." appears.*

King Fig. 167. Queen Fig. 168. Valet Fig. 169.

* Cartes a Jouer, Rene D' Allemagne.

Fig. 170*
THE EMPEROR, Atout No. 4. See page 33.
* Rene D'Allemagne.

Tarrochi by Gringonneur, cir. 1393.

In Paris are preserved seventeen beautifully painted cards which are said to be part of a pack specially designed and printed about 1393 by Jacquermin Gringonneur* for the amusement of Charles VI, the crazy king of France.

These seventeen cards probably formed part of a pack called Tarrochi cards (a complete pack of which is fifty). They are executed in the same style as seen in old illuminated missals, and are very beautifully finished by hand in gold, silver and colours. The gold background has been burnished with a pointed agate burnisher, the silver border being treated in the same way showing an intertwining dotted design. Some parts of the vestments and armour are heightened with gold and silver.

The cards are much larger than the ordinary modern ones, being 7½ in. by 3½ in.

An account of these seventeen cards is given by Mons. Duchesne, who connects them with the Atouts of the Tarot pack.

1. LE FOU—The Buffoon. (22). Fig. 37.
2. L'ECUYER—the Shield-Bearer.
**3. L'EMPEREUR—the Emperor. (4) Figs. 14 and 170.
4. LE PAPE—the Pope. (5). Fig. 15.
5. LES AMOUREUX—the Lovers. (6). Fig. 17.
6. LA FORTUNE—Fortune. (9). Fig. 22.
7. LA TEMPERANCE—Temperance. (15). Fig. 27.
8. LA FORCE—Fortitude. (12). Fig. 23.
9. LA JUSTICE—Justice. (8). Fig. 19.
10. LA LUNE—The Moon. (18). Figs. 32 and 171.

A line facsimile of this card is shown Fig. 171, It is evidently an emblem of astrology.

11. LE SOLIEL—the Sun. (19). Fig. 33.
12. LE CHAR—the Chariot. (7). Fig. 18.
13. L'ERMITE—the Hermit. (10). Fig. 20.
14. LE PENDU—the Hanged Man. (11). Fig. 25.
15. LE MORT—Death. (13). Fig. 26.
16. LE MAISON DIEU—The Hospital. (16). Fig. 30.
17. LE JUGEMENT DERNIER—the Last Judgement. (20). Fig. 34.

The figures in brackets are the numbers of the Atouts as generally used in the Tarot pack.†

* Page 22. ** Page 66. † Page 30

Fig. 171.

LA LUNE, Atout No. 18. See page 45.

Jacquermin Gringonneur, 1393.

Piquet Pack.

Two cards from a very dainty pack of *piquet* cards, having the ordinary suits, are shown in Figs. 172 and 173. The Coat cards are full length figures in elaborate costumes, and with the names of various characters as follows —

CLUBS.	THE KING "Bussy d'Amboise"
	THE QUEEN, "Dame de Monsoreau"
	THE VALET, a young man holding a horse.
HEARTS.	THE KING, Chevalier D'Eon.*
	THE QUEEN, Comtesse de Rochefort.
	THE VALET, a footman.
DIAMONDS.	THE KING, Fig. 172, Cinq-Mars.
	THE QUEEN, Marion Delorme.
	THE VALET, page with tray and glasses.
SPADES.	THE KING, Comte de Brissau.
	THE QUEEN, Fig. 173, Diane de Poitiers.
	THE VALET, page holding a greyhound.

All these cards are well designed, and neatly engraved and coloured, and are probably portraits of the characters named.

Each ace is enclosed in a nicely designed conventional frame.

Fig. 172.

Fig. 173.

* Chevalier D'Eon acted in a diplomatic capacity in several countries, was for a time Minister Plenipotentiary from France to London. He was affirmed in 1771 to be a female, and subsequently wore female attire, but at his death he was proved to be a male

Cir. 1832.

Fig. 176.

Fig. 177.

Fig. 178.

Fig. 179.

Cards for Col. Athalin, cir. 1832.

The Coat Cards belonging to a pack designed for Colonel Athalin, an officer in the Court of Louis Phillipe, are illustrated in "Cartes a Jouer."* They are clever open line drawings showing one of the principal episodes in the life of the hero who is represented.

The four Kings are :—

HEARTS.—CHARLEMAGNE, who is represented standing near a piece of gothic furniture, on which is placed the Imperial Crown which he has just received.

CLUBS—ALEXANDER is shown carrying his wounded father out from one of his battles.

DIAMONDS—CAESAR is leaning on the tomb of Alexander, the King of Macedonia upon whose bust he is gazing in ecstasy.

SPADES.—DAVID, who is shown with uplifted sword just about to cut off the head of Goliath.

The four Queens are :—

HEARTS—JUDITH, superbly clad carries a sword in her right hand, whilst with the left she grasps by the hair the head of Holofernes, which she has just cut off. Fig. 176.

CLUBS.—CLEOPATRA, who rather than be taken a prisoner to Rome, is seen ending her life by the poison of an asp, which she placed in her bosom. Fig. 177.

DIAMONDS—RACHAEL stands by the side of her cousin Jacob, who is lifting the heavy cover at the mouth of the well. Fig. 178.

SPADES.—PALLAS (the daughter of Jupiter) is represented standing with a shield and long spear, her breast covered with a coat of mail. At her feet amongst the branches is an owl. Fig. 179.

The four Knaves are :—

HEARTS—HARLEQUIN.

CLUBS.—GRINGONNEUR.†.

DIAMONDS—HECTOR. The Hero of the Trojans.

SPADES—HOGIER.

* Rene D'Allemagne. † Page 22.

Cartes a Rire, 19th Century.

(Cards to Amuse.)

Among the many packs of playing cards issued with the idea of amusing the players is one published by "*Grandebes, Rue de Richelieu, No. 91, Paris,*" under the title of "CARTES A RIRE." (*Cards to amuse*). These cards have upon them a series of cleverly drawn, fanciful and burlesque designs, attributed to *Baron Louis Atthalin,* in which the Kings and Queens personify the reactionary newspapers of the period.

Fig. 178.

Fig. 179.

THE KING OF DIAMONDS shows a large block with the head of a bearded man resting upon it. In the background is a figure of Father Time, and the name of the paper—"MONITEUR,"—which this card represents.

The King of Hearts appears as a Roman warrior with drawn sword and shield, standing by a column surmounted by a classical figure. The word "CONSTITUTIONNEL" is printed at the side of this card.

The Queen of Clubs shows an elderly lady, writing with a very large quill pen, and looking at a big bird in a cage, as if to gain inspiration from it. This is evidently intended to be a satire on the paper called the "GAZETTE."

Fig. 180.

In like manner the Queen of Hearts represents "MINERVE," the King of Clubs "DEBATS," the Queen of Spades "QUOTIDIENNE," and the King of Spades "CONSERVATEUR." The last named depicts a priest with a sword and flaming torch. On the Queen of Diamonds is printed "Lettres Normandes." The names on the four Valets are:—FIGARO (Hearts), CLOPINEAU (Clubs), DON QUICHOTTE (Diamonds), and BAZILE (Spades)'

The designs on the numeral cards are very carefully drawn. The two of Clubs Fig. 178, shows HEBE the goddess of youth, who waited upon the gods and filled their cups with nectar.

On the six of Clubs Fig. 179, ST. MICHEL is slaying the angel of darkness. Fig. 180 is the four of Spades on which are seen a Sultan and his Janissaire. Fig. 181, the nine of Spades, with the title "The Clever Animals," portrays a company of nine performing animals, some playing different instruments. The Donkey plays the spinet, the Pig the guitar, the Monkey the flageolet, and the other animals are dancing and singing.

The six of Hearts, Fig. 182, represents "Missionnaires," while the five of Diamonds shows a number of grotesque people who are dancing a minuet. The latter is obviously a piece of satire on an English ball, as it is entitled "Bal Anglais."

Fig. 181.

Fig. 182.

SPANISH CARDS.

Italy, France and Germany have each in turn claimed that playing cards were first invented or introduced into Europe by them. Spain, also, makes the same claim and bases the soundness of it upon the fact that "*Naipes,*" or "*Naijpes,*" (flat or level) the word used to denote cards in that country to-day is very similar to "Naibi" the name by which they were known in Italy about the end of the fourteenth century. The Abbe de la Rive maintains that they were introduced by the Spaniards who invaded Italy in 1282 under Peter III of Arragon.

It is also recorded that John I, King of Castille, in 1387 issued a command prohibiting "*game of dice Naypes* and Chess.*" This, it is argued, proves that cards were in use in Spain at a much earlier date, as gaming must have been well established before such a command could have been issued.

The cards used in Spain generally consist of a pack of forty-eight, the honours being King (Il Rey), Knight (Caballo—shown as a mounted horseman), and Knave (Sota). The numeral cards are one to nine, the tens being suppressed in each suit.

The Four Suits (see page 124), are *Swords* (*Espadas*), *Money,* (*Oras or Dineros*), *Cups* (*Copas*), and *Batons* (*Bastos*). These are the same suit signs as those used on the old Italian cards, but there are some interesting variations. For instance, while the Italian Kings are shown seated, the Spanish Kings are standing erect with their flowing robes covered with large ornaments, after the fashion of the French Kings. There is also a difference in the "pip" cards. The swords are straight two-edged ones, and the batons are rough, knotty branches of trees, sometimes shown vertically and sometimes horizontally, but not inter-laced in the inconvenient manner which generally prevails on the Italian tarot cards.

All Spanish playing cards are of the numeral kind, and tarot cards are unknown in Spain. In common with some Oriental, as well as German and Portuguese packs, there is no Queen, dame or woman among the honours cards.

Many of the packs are numbered in the top left-hand corner with the figures 1 to 12, and as there are no tens, the Knave, Knight and

* Page 207.

Fig. 183, Chevalier of Batons.

Fig. 184, Ace of Money.

Fig. 185, Four of Swords.

Fig. 186, Eight of Cups.

King are numbered 10, 11 and 12 respectively. A large proportion of the cards used in Spain are of very poor quality, the drawing and colouring being most crude and inartistic, but they are sold very cheaply. A notable exception, however, is a pack of forty-eight cards in the Author's collection, all of which are beautifully designed and coloured by hand. Fig. 187 is a facsimile in colour of the Ace of Cups, which shows a large cup or vase supported by two satyrs. The Ace of Money, Fig. 184, has upon it a large circular design, draped with a red mantle lined with ermine and surmounted by a crown. The Ace of Swords shows a very large sword in its scabbard with various flags and a quantity of armour. The Ace of Batons depicts two boys who are endeavouring to hold up the large branch of a tree. Fig. 183 shows the Chevalier of Batons.

On the fours the following clever designs are beautifully drawn and hand coloured :—

On Cups—Two cherubs each holding aloft a wine cup.

On Money—Four cherubs are seated around a table playing a game of cards.

On Swords—A cherub with a blazing torch is talking to Apollo (?), who is seated upon the ground. Fig. 185.

On Batons—A group of ten cherubs are dancing.

The eight of Cups is illustrated in Fig. 186.

France supplies Spain with a large quantity of playing cards, and this no doubt accounts for the fact that during the last few years some of the packs have borne the French suit signs of Cœurs (Hearts), Carreaux (Diamonds), Piques (Spades), and Trefles (Clubs), and sometimes a "Dame" is substituted for the Caballo.

A. Infirrira, 1694.

A pack of curious Spanish cards was published by A. Infirrira in 1694. Four of these are illustrated, and it will be seen how they appear to have been influenced by, if not actually copied from, oriental designs.

The dragon on each of the Aces is quite oriental in character, and the shields also resemble very closely those often seen on Hindostanee drawings.

Fig. 187, Ace of Cups.

Fig. 188.

Fig. 189.

The suit signs are Cups, Rings, Swords and Batons, and the coat cards are King, Queen and Caballero or Chevalier. It is very unusual to find a Queen on Spanish or Portuguese playing cards and the letters shown over the heads of the figures may indicate that they were printed in France,

Fig. 190.

Fig. 191.

R.S. would stand for Roi (or King) of Swords. Fig. 188.
D.S. would stand for Dame (or Queen) of Swords. Fig. 189.
C.S. would stand for Caballo of Swords. Fig. 190.
A.S. would stand for As (or Ace) of Swords. Fig. 191.

The Queen appears to be attacking a dragon in a very spirited manner, and on the Ace, the dragon has the sword in his mouth.

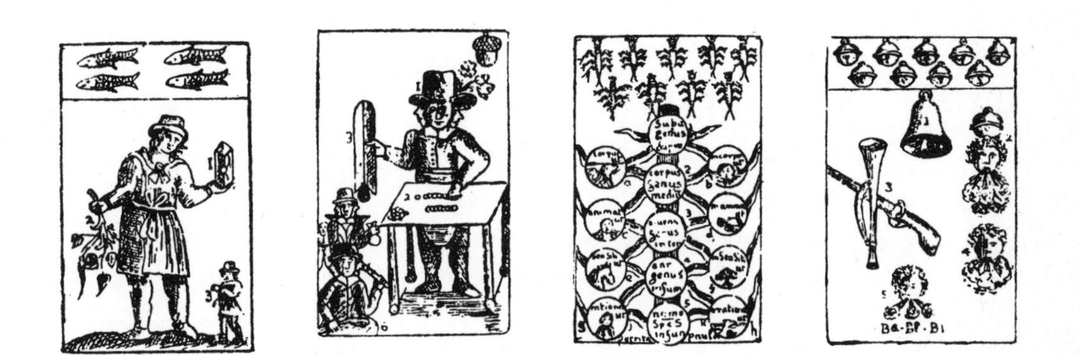

DUTCH, 1720.

A rare pack of fifty-two cards, with the ordinary suits of Hearts, Spades, Diamonds and Clubs, was published in Holland in 1720. In addition there are supplementary cards, on one of which a man is holding up a piece of drapery on which are the words :—

PASQUINS WINDKAART op de WINDNEGOTIE van't IAAR, 1720, the wording below referring to "the ghost of *Prince Frederick, &c.*" The other card shows a large strutting cock, and the inscription tells us "*these new bubble cards were made by Little Lau of the Scotch sign of the Goldseeking Cock.*"*

A series of clever engravings takes up the major portion of each of the fifty-two numeral cards, with explanatory wording below each one having some satirical reference to the South Sea and Mississippi bubble companies, both of which commenced in 1710 and burst in 1720, and brought ruin on thousands of families in England and France.

On the ACE OF HEARTS a tall gentleman appears to be trying to catch a mermaid, who is holding a mirror and who is seen half out of the water. In his right hand he holds a ring or hoop. Below is the following :—

"*De Zuidze Zesiereen dagt ik yet geefs te yangen—*
Zy knapt het geld, en laat de lage hengel hangen."

which may be translated thus :—

"*The Southern Mermaid I tried to catch in vain,*
She took the money and left me the empty hook."

The TWO OF CLUBS, Fig. 192, shows a gentleman who seems to be appealing to someone, and in the distance two men are fighting a duel.

Oh ! lay down your hands, the purse is empty. The furious brain has robbed many a man of Shares of property and blood."

The ACE OF DIAMONDS, Fig. 193, shows Samson wrestling with the lion :

Share Puzzle : Nothing so blind secret about the Shares was ever known before. The mysterious riddle of the brave Samson appeared."

The KING OF DIAMONDS, Fig. 194, shows a man behind some screens :—

I am protected when everyone squirms.
I am shielded from the winds blowing from the South and West. And a mild spirit helps the universe to slumber."

* This refers to John Law, author of the Mississippi Scheme.

Fig 192.

Fig. 193.

'k Ben voor de Zuid en West hun windgeblaas beschut
Terwyl een laauwe Geest 't Heel Al helpt in den dut.

Fig. 194.

Fig. 195.

The QUEEN OF SPADES, Fig. 195, shows a lady who is throwing away a number of cards.

"*The Spade is freely laid down, our games have been spoiled, the blind rage of Quimquampoix has ended.*"

The THREE OF SPADES, Fig. 196, shows one black and two white ladies seated on a large swing. The centre one holds a cord on the end of which a bird is attached.

"*See how the South and West and Mississippi swing on a spade, just as the wind drives them.*"

On the FOUR OF HEARTS, Fig. 197, we see a man who is dropping money into the mouth of a large fish :—

"*All goes to the sea, not to lose my money, by the shares, I throw it into the seas as bait for the fishes.*"

The Kings are named "Heer," the Queens "Vrouw," and the Knaves "Knegt."

Fig. 196.

Fig. 197.

BELGIAN.

Tarot Pack, cir. 1790.

A Tarot pack with the usual suit signs was published in Brussels by T. Servars, cir. 1790, but differs somewhat from the ordinary Atout pack, as twenty of the Atouts are shown as animals in place of the usual figures.

The Coat cards of this pack consist of King, Queen, Chevalier and Valet in each suit, making, with the numerals, fifty-six which added to the twenty-two Atouts make seventy-eight. The figures are fairly well drawn, but badly coloured by means of a stencil. The four Kings, all crowned and holding sceptres, are standing in a defiant attitude. The four Queens have their dresses trimmed with ermine, and each one is holding a sceptre. The four Chevaliers are on horses, and those on Hearts and Spades are holding pistols, while the one on Diamonds is dressed as a huntsman. The Chevalier of Clubs appears to be addressing someone and he has a religious picture embroidered on his under-coat. The Valets of Diamonds and Spades hold axes, and the Valet of Hearts Fig. 199 has a banner, while the Valet of Clubs has a sword and a long staff. Fig. 198. shows the King of Diamonds.

As stated, peculiarity of this pack is the way in which the Atout cards differ from the ordinary Atouts, as they consist for the most part, of animals instead of the usual emblematic figures. On No. 1 a man is dancing and holding in his left hand a glass of wine or ale, but on Nos. 2 to 21 the following animals are found portrayed :—

2	Stag	8	Unicorn	15	Turtle
3	Dog	9	Wild Boar	16	Frog
4	Camel	10	Bison (?)	17	Cat
5	Wolf	11	Lion	18	Donkey
6	Fox	12	Monkey	19	Sheep
7	Rabbit	13	Crocodile	20	Goat
		14	Beaver (?)	21	Bear

The Fou or Mat on the 22nd card is shown as a man playing on a flute.

Belgian.

Fig. 198.

Fig. 199

English, 17th Century

Fig. 200.

Fig. 201.

ENGLISH CARDS

Old English 17th Century.

The Knave of Clubs, Fig. 200 and Queen of Hearts, Fig. 201, on page 132 are from an English pack which was found in an old Stuart cabinet. They had been used for winding various colours of wool or silk upon them and the name of the colours being written on the back of the card. The maker's name, "C. HEWSON," on Fig. 200, shows they date back to the end of the 17th century, and this is verified by a piece of vellum wrapped around one of the cards with the name "*Hannah Boulton,*" and date 1682, and stating that this is

"*her shade of white for her hair.*"

The Queens of Hearts, Spades and Diamonds are holding a flower, but the Queen of Clubs has a Squirrel seated upon her left hand.

Educational.

Compendium of Geography, cir. 1790.

This is a pack of 52 cards, with the usual suits, Hearts, Diamonds, Spades and Clubs, shown at the top left-hand corner in a space about ¾ in. square, the rest of the card being closely printed with particulars of various countries pertaining to the four great continents. Hearts are for Europe, Clubs for Africa, Spades for Asia and Diamonds for America.

An extra card gives full particulars as to the use of the pack, thus :—

PREFACE.

" While Guthrie's and other grammars instruct those only who have the opportunity for study ; this compendium is calculated to give those who have not much time to read, (and particularly young persons at school) a general acquaintance with the bigness, boundaries,* population, capitals, lat. and lon distance from London, islands, rivers, lakes, mountains, climates, productions, agriculture, manufactures, trades, government, religion, customs, learning, and curiosities of every kingdom or state in the world, in an easy, sausory manner; as it describes Asia under spades, Africa under clubs, Europe under hearts and America under diamonds; arranged thus, each quarter is described on the first page of its suit, and each K. page contains the kingdoms, and the number pages their description ; the reader will observe that

Tartary on the K. of spades, has the figure 2 annexed, which refers to the 2 of spades; England, Scotland and Ireland, have 2, 3, 4, their description begins on the 2, & ends on the 4, &c. the islands are on the Q. & J. of each suit."

Should the scientific discover any inaccuracies, their candour will ascribe them to some pardonable cause; & that of the public will graciously accept the labours of the Author, as an evidence of his good-will towards mankind.

*B. stands for bounded, N. for North, &c. O. for Ocean, R. for River, M. for Miles.

[Entered as the Act directs.]

INDOSTAN, B. N. Usbec Tartary and Thibet, S. Bay of Bengal, E. Asem. Ava, and Pegu. W. Indian O. and Persia, from Lon. 3720 m. S. E. The winds blow 6 months one way and then 6 the other., and in April, May and June very hot. Mahometan princes made conquests here as early as the 7th century, & established the Mogul empire, which now extends its jurisdiction over two populous and extended empires of India, which. united, go under the title of Indostan, part of which is gov'rned by Indian Kings, subject to the great Mogul, an absolute monarch. Tho' some parts are mountainous, sandy and barren, yet, in general, it is a level, well-watered, rich and vastly fertile country, producing every comfort & luxury of life; and their commerce is courted by all the world: from hence the Greeks and Romans drew their highest materials of luxury; and it was not unknown, even in Solomon's time. It is divided into a number of provinces, that in the gulf of Cambaya, is one of the finest in India, contains 35 cities. Abed, the capital, is said to vie in wealth with any town in Europe. Agra contains 40 towns and 340 villages; at Delhi is the imperial palace with all the eastern magnificence; Tatta the cap. of Sindia, is famous for manufactures; the province of Casimere is a mere paradise, contains 100,000 villages stored with cattle and game. The province of Bengal is the store-house of the Indies, its fertility exceeds Egypt. On both sides of the Ganges are canals cut 100 miles, on which are towns, cities and castles, among which the English, Dutch, and French have many factories and great possessions. Rel. Mahom. and Pagan. The males marry at 14, and females at 11; a man declines at 30, and a woman is old at 25. The people of Indostan carry on a Trade to Mecca; and a Mahometan junk or vessel returning from its voyage, is often worth 300,000 l. such is the riches of the country, that Europeans are continually seeking their trade, and getting possessions here.

Fig. 202.

ENGLAND, Wales and Scotland, form an island, and go under the name of Great-Britain, B. N. Northern O. S. Eng. Chan. & Atlan. E. Ger. O. W. St. George's Chan. Ireland is an island, and lies in the Atlan. is divided into 3 provinces, viz. Ulster, Leinster and Connaught, which are sub-divided into 32 counties, the principal towns, of which are Dublin, containing 221000 inha. Cork 87000, Limerick 32000, Waterford 18500, Londonderry 18000, Belfast 15500, Newry 3500, Galway 9000, Roscommon 8000, tho' incumbered with bogs and morasses; yet in general it is level, fruitful, well-watered country; its harbours, rivers and bays, give it great advantage in trade. In beef, butter, cheese and linen manufactures it equals Eng. Scotland divided into 12 counties, the principal towns of which are Edinburgh, containing 98000 inha Glasgow 50000, Aberdeen 18000, Inverness 11000, Paisley 6000, Dumfries 5000; tho' a great part is mountainous and barren; yet by industry and their knowledge of agriculture, it is made a pretty plentiful country. England is divided into 40 counties, and Wales into 12, the principal towns of which are London, 1000000 inh. York 100000, Bristol 85000, Birmingham 58000, Liverpool 44000, Newcastle 42000, Norwich 41500, Manchester 38000, Worcester 23000, Leeds 22500, Hull 20000, Exeter 20000, Nottingham 20000, Bath 17000, and when full 9000 more, Chester 16000, Halifax 1500, Shrewsbury 15000, Coventry 15000, Oxford 12000, University 2500 more, Salisbury 10000, Cambridge 7000, University 1500 more. The climate of England is mild, the soil naturally very good, yielding every useful production, excepting wine, oil, and silk. The genius and industry of the people in the arts of agriculture and gardening, in the mode of feeding cattle, breeding horses and sheep, have placed them in the first rank of European countries. Their cheese and malt liquors are in high estimation; but their wool is their grand staple; their mines also are great

Fig. 203.

The four of Spades Fig. 202, gives particulars of India, or INDOSTAN, as it is spelt on this card. The two of Hearts Fig. 203 tells us all about Great Britain, the particulars of which take up the whole of three cards, viz.:—the two, three and four of Hearts. On each of the King cards we have the countries enumerated, with their length, breadth, number of inhabitants, the latitude and longitude, and capital town. On each of the Queen and Knave Cards particulars of the Islands are given with the soil and produce, as for instance, on the Queen of Clubs, we are told the Azores are very fertile in corn, wine and fruits. And on the Knave of Spades we read that Sumatra is 1000 miles by 100 miles, and lies under the equator, and produces much pepper and so much gold that " 'tis tho't to be the ancient Ophir."

The "honours" cards are indicated by the letters K, for King, Q. for Queen, and J. for Jack placed on the suit marks in the top left-hand corner. They are also ornamented with flowers, crowns, birds, lions, &c.

A few interesting extracts :—

Seven of Diamonds, describing the state of New York, says:—

"It has several fine cities and towns," but New York is the cap. where is a University, which, it is expected, will soon flourish."

Nine of Hearts (Italy)

"Mount Etna issues such rivers of melted minerals as destroys whole towns, and 12,000 persons at once."

Four of Clubs (Egypt).

"Relig. Mahom., and tho'it was once the seat of arts and sciences, there scarce remains a vestige of it among the present inhabitants."

Ten of Diamonds (Peru).

"In 1612, to receive one of the governors in pomp, they paved the streets of Lima with silver and it is amazing to behold the churches decorated with gold, silver, and precious stones."

Three of Clubs (Morocco.)

"500 miles by 470 miles. Its government can scarcely be said to exist."

Seven of Spades (Arabia)

"The Arabs are descendants of Ishmael and are a robbing, thieving people."

Fig. 204.

Astronomical, 1676.

In the endeavours to impart knowledge by means of playing cards Astronomy has not been forgotten. In 1676 a pack was advertised to be sold by the author, Joseph Moxon (Hydrographer to the King's most Excellent Majesty) on Ludgate Hill, at the sign of the Atlas, the advertisement relating to them reading as follows —

"The use of Astronomical playing cards teaching any ordinary capacity by them to be aquainted with all the stars of Heaven, to know their place in Heaven, Colour, Nature, and Bigness; as also the Poetical Reasons for every Constellation; very useful present and delightful for all lovers of ingenuity."

Two cards from this pack are illustrated. On the three of Hearts, Fig. 205 we have the constellation of "GEMINI" (*The Twins*). One is holding a spear and the other has a reaping hook. A large star is marked *Castor* and at the bottom, the date on which it sets is given as "Decemb. 19, N.E."

The Ace of Diamonds, Fig. 205 shows the constellation "DRACO" (*The Dragon*) and we are told that it "Sets not."

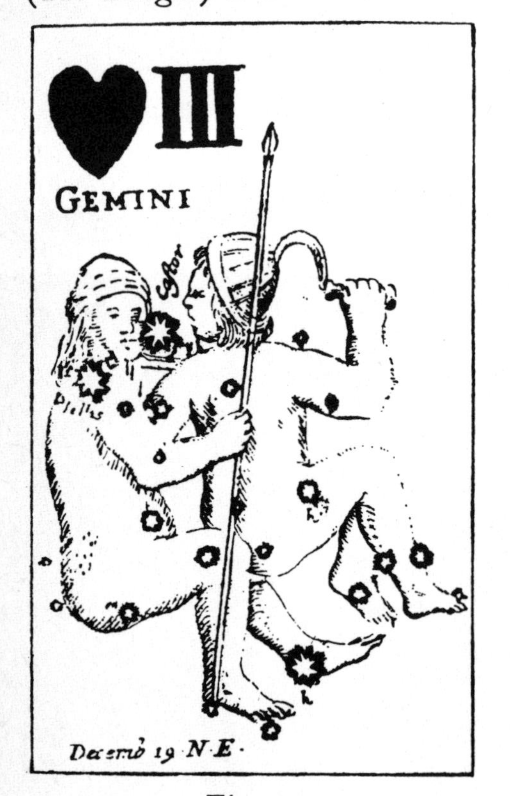

Fig. 205.

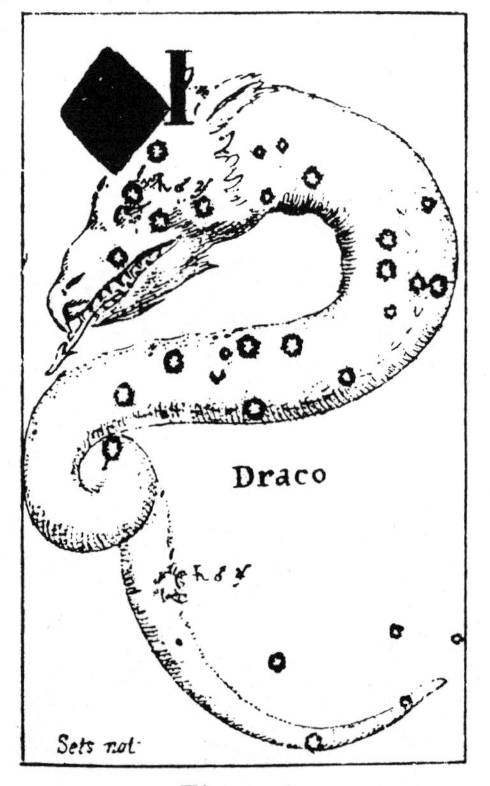

Fig. 206.

The Constellations on some of the other cards are:—
King of Hearts—LEO (*The Lion*), Feb. 6, E.N.E.
Ace of Hearts—URSA MAJOR (*The Great Bear*), Sets not.
Two of Hearts—CANCER (*The Crab*). Decemb. 8, N.E. by E.
Three of Diamonds—HERCULES. April 8, N.E. by E.
Seven of Diamonds—SCORPIO (*The Scorpion*). May 23, S.E.
Four of Spades—TAURUS (*The Bull*). Nov. 28, E.N.E.

The Medallions on the four Kings are probably portraits of Charles II.

Astronomical, cir. 1825.

Another pack of Astronomical cards, published by C. HODGES, Portman Square, about 1825, are very carefully engraved, and beautifully finished in colours, the Coat cards especially being very artistic. They represent the following mythological gods and goddesses.

SPADES.	NEPTUNE.	VENUS.	SATURN.
HEARTS.	JUPITER.	JUNO.	MERCURY.
DIAMONDS.	MARS.	MINERVA.	VULCAN.
CLUBS.	BACCHUS.	DIANA.	APOLLO.

Three of the signs of the Zodiac are placed on each suit as follows:—

SPADES.	PISCES.	CAPRICORNUS.	AQUARIUS.
HEARTS.	TAURUS.	GEMINI.	ARIES.
DIAMONDS.	LEO.	VIRGO.	CANCER.
CLUBS.	SCORPIO.	LIBRA.	SAGITTARIUS.

ORION is on the four of Diamonds.
URSA MAJOR on the seven of Diamonds.
HERCULES on the seven of Clubs.
PEGASUS on the six of Spades.
AESTAS on the ace of Diamonds.
ANDROMEDA on the four of Spades.
ARGO NAVIS on the six of Clubs.
AURIGA on the five of Hearts.

Every card in this pack is worth studying, not only for its historical, but also for its artistic value. They are beautifully finished in coours similar to Fig. 207 in the Geographical pack by the same maker.

Fig. 207, Empress of Austria.

Fig. 208.

Fig. 209.

Geographical, cir. 1820.

A very artistic pack of 52 Geographical Cards was published about 1820 by C. Hodges of 27 Portman Street, Portman Square, who represents the four suits as Europe (Hearts), Asia (Diamonds), Africa (Clubs), and America (Spades). The Court cards, which are very finely engraved and beautifully finished in gold and colours, are representative of various countries in each continent.

HEARTS (Europe).

King	George III of England.
Queen.	Empress of Austria. Fig. 207, facsimile.
Knave.	Frenchman trampling on the crown and sceptre, and holding aloft the Cap of Liberty.

DIAMONDS (Asia).

King.	Chinese Mandarin.
Queen.	Eastern Lady.
Knave.	Arab.

CLUBS (Africa).

King.	Egyptian, holding golden rod.
Queen.	Algerian Lady (?).
Knave.	Gentleman of Morocco, with long pipe.

SPADES (America).

King.	President of the United States.
Queen.	South American lady with child.
Knave.	Red Indian.

Each of the aces of the numeral cards has upon it a map of one of the continents, Fig. 209 shows Africa on Ace of Clubs while on the cards numbered two to ten of each suit are maps of the various countries. Here are two from each suit as example:—

5 of Hearts . .	Italy.	7 of Clubs . .	Abyssinia.
10 of Hearts, Fig. 208.	British Isles.	10 of Clubs . . .	Egypt.
2 of Diamonds . .	Japan.	4 of Spades. . .	Chili.
8 of Diamonds .	Hindostan.	9 of Spades. .	Canada.

English Counties, cir. 1680.

The realisation of the fact that there are 52 counties in England and Wales evidently gave someone living in the reign of Charles II (about 1680) the idea that a map of a county placed on each card would help in the study of Geography. Two extra cards are issued with the 52 counties, on one of which is the wording "A Mapp of England and Wales," and a map engraved with the 52 counties marked upon it, on the other are instructions how to use the cards.

The King in each suit is no doubt intended as a portrait of Charles II, Fig. 210, while Catherine of Braganza represents on each suit the queens. The Queen of Clubs is on the County of Durham' Fig. 211 the Queen of Spades on Radnor, the Queen of Hearts on Huntington, and the Queen of Diamonds on Worcester Sh.

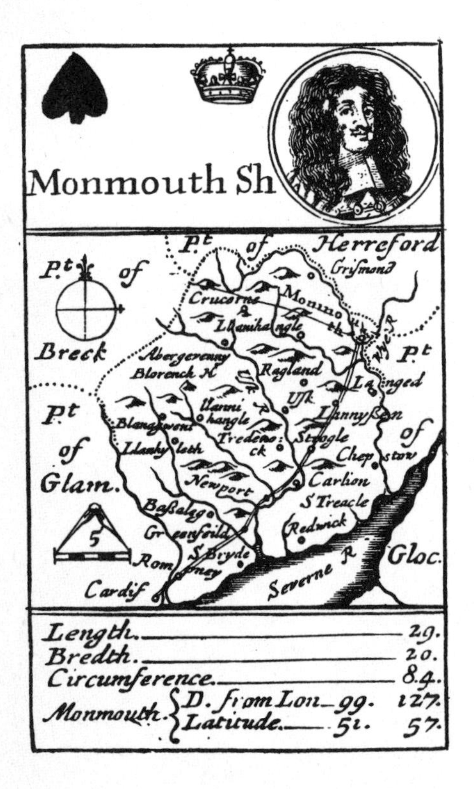

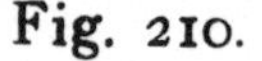
Fig. 210.

Fig. 211.

The Knaves on each suit are different.

The Knave of Clubs on Rutland shows a simple-looking man wearing a coat buttoned up to his neck and a hat fashioned like a night cap with a tassel.

The Knave of Spades on Anglesey is a jolly, laughing man with long wavy hair, open collar, and broad brimmed hat with a large feather.

The Knave of Hearts on Lecester Sh., shows in profile a strong, intelligent looking man with dark, wavy hair.

The Knave of Diamonds on Glocester Sh., shows a gentleman with long hair, pointed beard and long moustache, whose hand is upraised as if in debate. Fig. 212.

The King of Clubs is on the county of York Sh., the King of Spades on Monmouth Sh., Fig. 210 the King of Hearts on Hereford Sh., and the King of Diamonds on Middlesex.

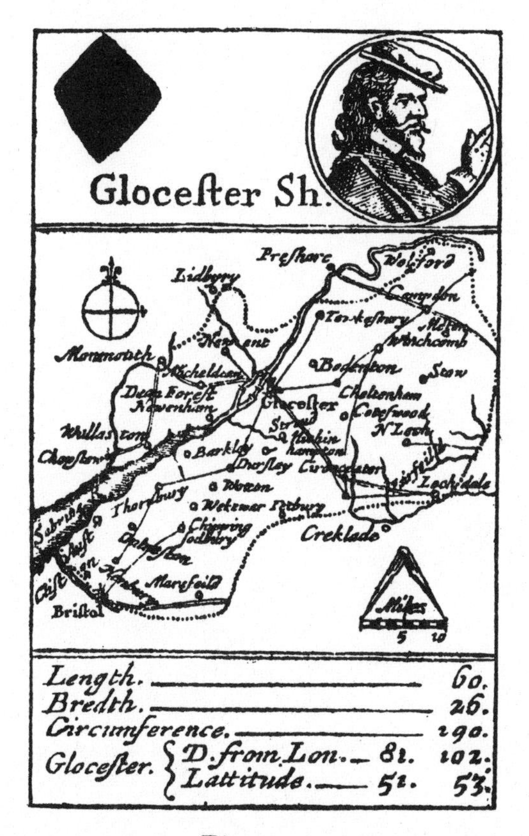

Fig. 212.

Fig. 213.

The Pip cards are on the following counties :—

CLUBS.

Ace—Westmorland.
2—Cumberland.
3—Lancaster Sh.
4—Cheshire.
5—Darby Sh.
6—Northumberland.
7—Nottingham Sh.
8—Hartford Sh.
9—Stafford Sh.
10—Shrop Shire.

DIAMONDS.

Ace—Warwick Sh.
2—Oxford Sh. Fig. 213.
3—Barke Sh.
4—Sussex.
5—Hant Sh.
6—Wilt Sh.
7—Dorset Sh.
8—Somerset Sh.
9—Devon Sh.
10—Cornwall.

HEARTS.

Ace—Northampton Sh.
2—Buckingham Sh.
3—Bedford Sh.
4—Cambridge Sh.
5—Norfolk.
6—Suffolk.
7—Essex.
8—Lincoln Sh.
9—Kent.
10—Surrey.

SPADES.

Ace—Flint Shire
2—Carnarvan.
3—Denbigh Sh.
4—Merioneth Sh.
5—Montgomery Sh.
6—Cardigan Sh.
7—Brecknok Sh.
8—Glamorgan Sh.
9—Carmarthen Sh.
10—Pembroke Sh.

Under each map is given particulars of the county it represents Taking Oxfordshire see Fig. 213 as an example.

	Length . .	41
	Bredth . .	29
	Circumference .	144
Oxford	Distance from London	47–55
	Latitude . . .	51–46

To Teach the Alphabet, cir. 1675.

A pack of cards published about 1675, was evidently intended as a help in teaching the Alphabet. They are engraved in open line from wood blocks, and each card has an oval design surrounded by figures of cupids, birds, mermaids, serpents, &c., intertwined with a conventional flowing ornamentation. Above this oval there is a square space containing the suit marks and values. The idea is, apparently to show the various forms of letters, and three kinds are illustrated, viz. :—Black letter 𝔑. 𝔫., Roman, N n., and Italic, *N. n.,* as shown on the Three of Clubs Fig. 214. On some of the cards in the suit of Diamonds, there are syllables of two letters. On the Five, Fig. 215, we find ab, eb, ib, ob, ub and on the Eight af, ef, if, of, uf, and so on.

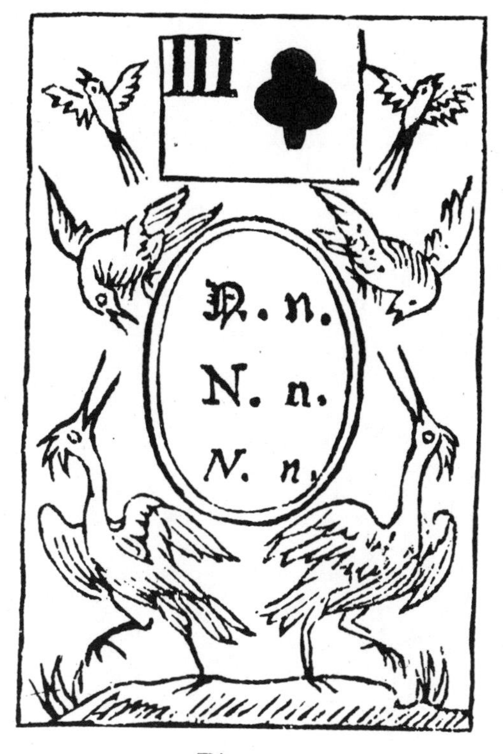

Fig. 214.

Fig. 215.

The ovals on the Coat cards contain more moral teaching, as seen on the Queen of Clubs, Fig. 216, where we read :.—

" Cards may be used, but not abused
And they used well, All games Exell."

On King of Hearts—

" A trusty heart suits to a King
And subjects true in everything."

On Knave of Spades—

" A Gamester that Doth Play for Game,
Is but a knave and that is Plaine."

On Queen of Spades—

" Where Queens by Vertue : truely swaide
No Eveill can theire Minds Invade."

On 3 of Diamonds—

" These Cards were truly well Designed
To Ground all Letters in Youths Minde."

On 4 of Diamonds—

" Both Youth and Age may learne hereby :
All Sorts of Letters Speedily."

Fig. 216.

To teach Latin, cir. 1676.

A pack of fifty-two cards with the ordinary suits was published about 1676 with the object of teaching the rules of grammar and furnishing help in the study of Latin, all the instructions which are printed on the cards being in that language. The suit of Spades teaches

Fig. 217.

Fig. 218.

"ORTHOGRAPHIA," that of Clubs "ETYMOLGIA," the suit of Hearts "SYNTAXIS," and Diamonds "PROSOBIA." The player is informed that "*All games may be played thereon with witty jests, sweet flowing Latine and great understanding.*" The cards are engraved from wood blocks and are of inferior character.

Another pack, probably published in Holland, with the same idea of teaching Latin, has the ordinary suit numbers placed in small circles at the bottom of each card, but there are four other signs which might be taken for suits. Thus on Clubs we have Marigolds, where the King, Fig. 216, is shown holding a scroll with words *"Deus, Meus, Iesus."*

Fig. 219. Fig. 220.

The signs on Spades are bunches of grapes. The Ace, Fig. 218, shows two men bending beneath the weight of a very large bunch of grapes, probably a reference to the Bible story of the spies.*

On Diamonds, Fig. 129, which shows the five, a geometrical design is used, while Hearts has a square-shaped shield on which are Latin words and sentences as seen in Fig. 220, which shows the two.

The four designs are repeated on the cards from one to ten, and are also shown on the Coat cards. See Fig. 217.

To teach Heraldry, 1684.

A pack was designed and published by Richard Blome in 1684 for the purpose of assisting students in Heraldry. This was one of many packs brought out to impart, in a pleasant manner, knowledge on various subjects. On each of these fifty-two cards are engraved illustrations of the principles of heraldry, all properly emblazoned.

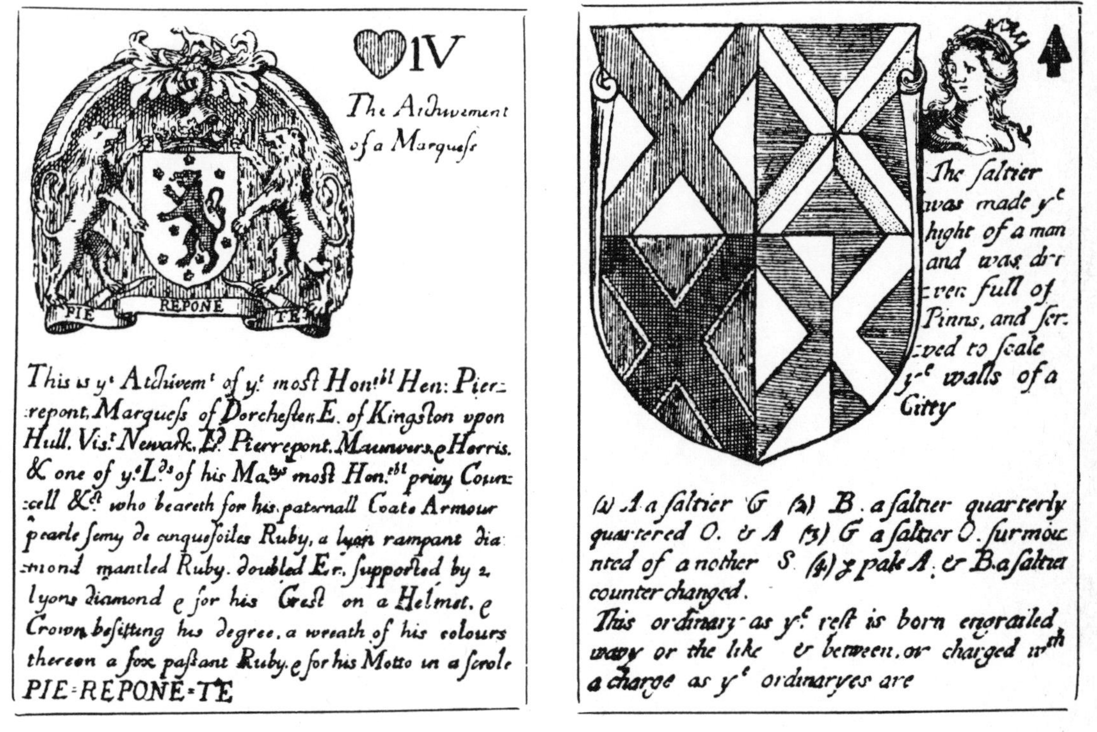

Fig. 221. Fig. 222.

The four of Hearts Fig. 221 gives the arms of "*Ye most Hon'bl. Hen : Pierrepont, Marquess of Dorchestor, E. of Kingston upon Hull, etc.*" It is emblazoned thus —"Ruby, a lyon rampant, mantled Ruby doubled Er., supported by a lyon, for his Crest on a Helmet a Crown befitting his degree, a wreath of his colours thereon a fox passant Ruby and for his motto on a scrole '*Pie-Repone-Te,* i.e., 'Repose with pious confidence.' "

On the Queen of Spades Fig. 222, are particulars relating to the use of the saltier. We are told that "*The Saltier was made ye hight of a man and was driven full of Pinns, and served to scale ye walls of a Citty.*"

The King of Hearts has engraved upon it the Royal Arms and a portrait of Charles II with the wording :—"*The Royall Atchievement of his Sacred Ma'ty Charles by ye Grace of God, King of England, Scotland France, Ireland, defender of ye faith.*"

Then follows the full emblazon of the King's arms, etc. :—
On the Ace and Two of Hearts, "Military Things."
Knave of Hearts, "Navall Things."
Five, Six, and Seven, the Achievement of an "Earle," a "Viscount," and a "Baron" respectively.

On the other cards are particulars of the Roundel, Countercharge, Pile, Chevron, Monsters, and Birds.

The illustration on the King of Hearts is no doubt a portrait. It is the same as that on a pack of Geographical Cards, described on page 140, which were published in 1680. See Fig. 210.

Fig. 223.

Fig. 223, One of the oldest caricatures known (cir. 1498) represents a political game of cards in progress. The King of France, Louis XII is seated, and around the table we have Pope Alexander VI, (Roderic Borgia) who was poisoned by drinking from a bowl he had prepared for another, Henry VII of England, distinguished by the three armorial lions on his breast, the Doge of Venice, Count Palatine and others.

Transformation Cards, cir. 1810.

This is an English pack, issued about 1810, of the suits Hearts, Spades, Diamonds and Clubs. These cards are treated in a humorous manner and in some cases are not very refined. The marks of the suits are made to fit into various parts of the figures, with exclamations relating to what they are supposed to be saying or doing. The six of clubs is entitled "Englishman in Paris," and a lady and gentleman are pictured at dinner in a restaurant. The gentleman holds up a frog on his fork and addresses a waiter, who replied "*Ils sont les veritables Grenouilles, monsieur.*" To which the gentleman replies, "*Green owls, damme ; they're nothing but Frogs.*" Fig. 228.

Fig. 224. Fig. 225.

The two of diamonds shows a lady followed by a gentleman, in a very high wind (as suggested by the bending trees and the lady's dress). He is saying :—

"*O take me to your arms, my love,*
For keen the wind doth blow."

She replies :—

"*Begone, you dirty fellow,*
How dare you use me so."

Fig. 226.

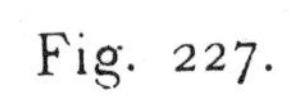

Fig. 227.

Fig. 228.

On Fig. 226 the Ace of Clubs forms the head and face of a rather ferocious-looking armed bandit or smuggler, who is watching a vessel which is just off the land. He is described on the card as "*Three Finger'd Jack.*"*

On the four of Hearts a gentleman is seen bowing to a lady and saying "*Madam, I am eternally yours,*" to which the lady replies, "*Are you in earnest, Sir* "

The Seven of Clubs shows us "*Miss Priscilla Prickfinger, Milliner and Fancy-dress Maker,*" who, with three other young ladies, is very busy with her needle. Fig. 225.

The designs are generally of a common description, except those on the Court cards which are much better drawn and are whole-length figures of a conventional form.

In the diamonds and hearts the faces are human, but of a grotesque character, In clubs the King has the head of a bull, the Queen the head of an owl, and the Knave the head of a ram. In spades the King has the head of an ape, the Queen the head of a cat Fig. 224, and the Knave the head of a dog. Each of the court cards is enclosed in a border ornamented with a number of small cards.

The name "Cowell" (the designer) is etched on some of the cards.

* A character in the pantomime of "Obi," which first appeared in 1800.

Transformation Cards, 1828.

A pack of 52 cards, designed by an artist named Olivatte, and printed from wood blocks was published January, 1828. The numerals are cleverly worked into the designs, as shown on page 153, where five cards from this pack are illustrated.

On the Ace of Clubs is printed:—

London
F. Olivatte, 6 Leigh Strt, Burton Crescent,
1st Jany 1828.

The pips on the THREE OF CLUBS Fig. 229 are made to form the bodies of a gentleman and two ladies, to whom he is reading.

Fig. 230 shows a group of Cherubs at play, their wings forming the Four of Diamonds.

The pips on the TWO OF CLUBS Fig. 231 form the heads of two little negro boys with bow and arrow.

The pips on the THREE OF SPADES Fig. 233 are cleverly introduced as the windows, &c., of a church.

It will be thus seen that many of the pip cards of this pack have a vein of humour in them, but the twelve Coat cards are on quite different lines, as they are represented by characters taken from Greek history.

On the KNAVE OF HEARTS, Fig. 232, we have "*Ulysses,*" who seems to be offering a petition to someone. He was one of the principal Greek heroes in the Trojan war, and his wonderful adventures are related by Homer in his "Odyssey."

On the KING OF CLUBS is "*Menelaus,*" whom Homer, describes as a man of athletic figure, and says of him that he spoke little but what he said was always impressive. His wife was the beautiful Helene, for whose sake the ten years Trojan war was fought, and who is shown as Queen of Clubs.

On the KING OF SPADES we find "*Agamemnon,*" who, Homer tells us, was the most powerful prince of Greece.

Homer himself, the great epic poet of Greece, is represented as the KNAVE OF DIAMONDS.

On the Queen of Hearts we have "*Penelope,*" the wife of Ulysses, who is shown in armour and with a drawn sword.

Fig. 229, Three of Clubs

Fig. 230, Four of Diamonds.

Fig. 231, Two of Clubs.

Fig. 232, Knave of Hearts.

Fig. 233, Three of Spades.

The Queen of Spades is represented by "*Clytemnestre*" (the mother of Atlas and Prometheus), who is weeping at a tomb.

Other characters represented on the Coat cards are, on the Knave of Spades "*Egiste,*" on the King of Diamonds "*Priam*" (King of Troy), Knave of Clubs "*Eneas,*" and the King of Hearts "*Polypheme.*"

All the Court cards are hand-coloured. Another pack (early 19th century), illustrated on page 89, is on the same lines as the above, but is much better finished and coloured.

A number of packs on similar lines were produced in France, Germany, and England in the 18th and early in the 19th centuries, many of them bearing designs of an indecent and gross character. Recently America has also produced packs where the pips are more or less cleverly incorporated into the drawings, but they are mostly of the comic kind.

Transformation Cards, 1818.

The cards illustrated on page 155 are from a very artistic pack published in 1818 in connection with the "Repository of Arts." They were issued four at a time, and were designed by a Viennese artist, Herr Osiander. The designing, drawing and engraving are very fine and most carefully executed, in a mezzo-tint, much after the style of many of Bartolozzi's engravings.

The subjects are very varied, as may be judged by Fig. 236, where the five of Spades is very cleverly worked into the design, which shows a group of people, one of whom appears to be giving a toast. Also on the three of Clubs, Fig. 237, we have a pleasing little homely design, with the three pip signs very ingeniously worked into the cradle, furniture, &c.

To give an idea of the marvellous and charming variety, the whole of the cards should be seen, as they comprise illustrations of soldiers fighting, worshippers before their altars, duels and tournaments, humorous pantomime and dramatic scenes, ladies playing on various musical instruments, mythological and love scenes, &c. This is one of the cleverest of the many packs of a similar kind.

The Coat cards are full length figures and are probably intended to represent historical or classical characters, but they are not named. They are coloured by hand, and Fig. 235 (The King of Clubs) and Fig. 234 (The Queen of Hearts) are reproduced in facsimile from the original cards.

Fig. 234.

Fig. 235.

Fig. 236.

Fig. 237.

Caricature Pack.

During the reign of George IV a number of caricature packs were published and Fig. 238 shows a card taken from one of these, where the five of Spades represents a circus acrobat, with the following wording :—

" *The celebrated Signior Pietro Francisco Joseph Andrea Balanca, First Equilibrist to His Catholic Majesty.*"

Other cards from this pack are shown in various characters. The five of Clubs is a drunken harlequin, the four of Hearts shows a butcher's shop with two dogs running off with two hearts. The Queen of Clubs is a lady who is belabouring her husband with a rolling pin. Cupid is shown on the Knave of Hearts, the Knave of Spades is a Sexton, and the King of Spades is a gardener. Venus represents the Queen of Hearts.

The designs are well drawn, and full of life, but the humour is generally rather poor.

Fig. 238.

Aſtrology, cir. 1640.

A pack of fifty-two cards, with an additonal two describing their use, was published about 1640, These cards have the ordinary suit marks and values printed at the top of each one, and the values on the Coat cards are given in Roman numerals, the Knave being XI, the Queen XII and the King XIII.

The names on the Coat cards are as follows :—

SUIT.	KING.	QUEEN.	KNAVE.
DIAMONDS.	NIMROD.	PROSERPINA.	MAHOMETT.
CLUBS.	PHAROAH.	CLYTEMNESTRA.	HEWSON.
HEARTS.	HEROD.	SEMIRAMIS.	CUPID. .
SPADES.	HOLOPHERNES.	DIDO.	WAT TYLER, Fig. 240.

The 1, 3, 5, 7 and 9 of Diamonds, the 1, 3, 5, 7 and 9 of Hearts, and the 1 and 5 of Spades carry the twelve signs of the Zodiac. Fig. 239 shows the five of Diamonds and the sign "Gemini," and eight other cards have the circle but with cabaliſtic signs, myſtical numbers and charaĉters.

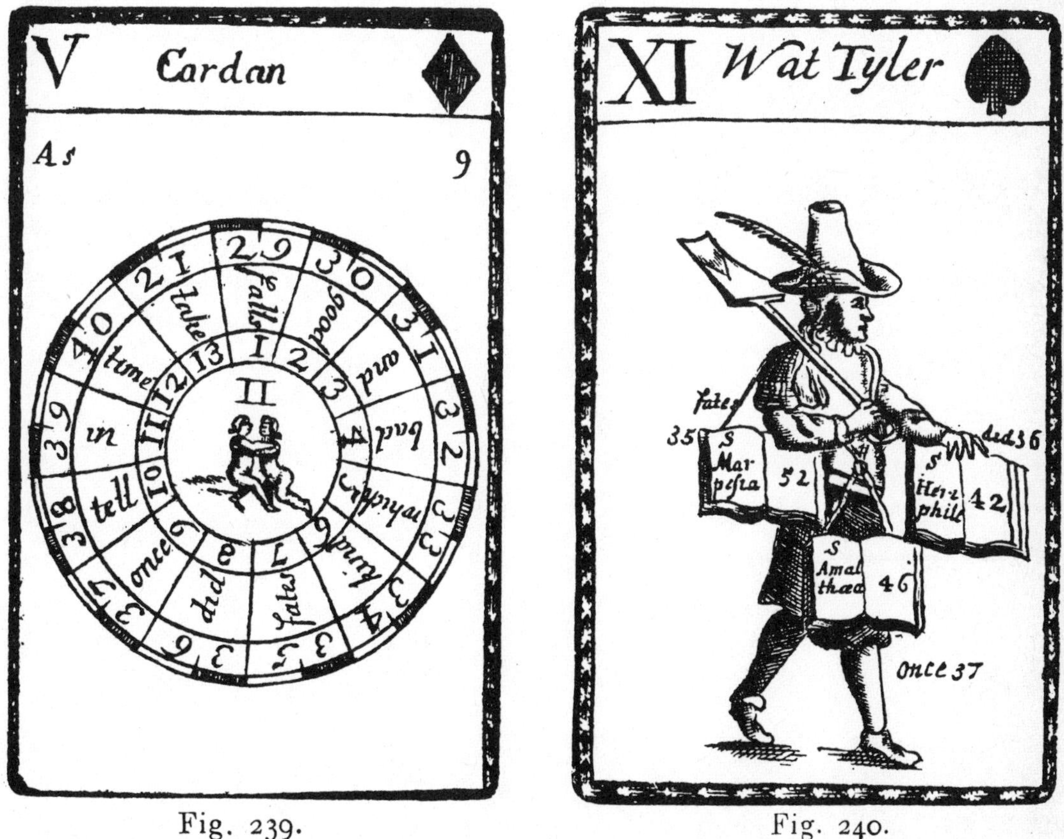

Fig. 239. Fig. 240.

The pack was no doubt intended to be used for fortune-telling, and on the 2, 4 6, 8 and 10 of each suit are thirteen lines of prophecy which are evidently intended to answer the questions shown upon the four Kings. See King of Clubs Fig. 241.

Here are a few examples from the 265 lines of answers which are found on the 2, 4, 6, 8 and 10 of each suit :— Fig. 242, IIII of Spades.

This year I see you'l marry'd be.
Of Gentil state shall be your Mate.
Children you'l have, most for the Grave.
There's three or two, in store for you. Fig. 242.

The two extra cards give instructions and also an example showing how to use the cards in order to look into the future.

Fig. 241.

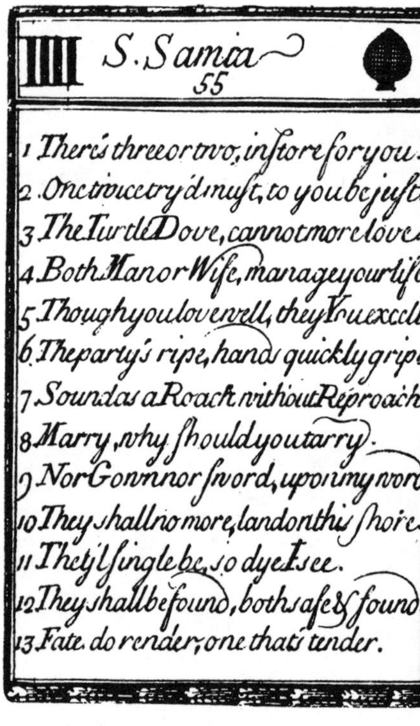

IIII S. Samia
55

1 There's three or two, in store for you.
2 One twice try'd must, to you be just.
3 The Turtle Dove, cannot more love.
4 Both Man or Wife, manage your life
5 Though you love well, they you excell
6 The party's ripe, hand quickly gripe
7 Sound as a Roach without Reproach
8 Marry, why should you tarry.
9 Nor Gonn nor sword, upon my word
10 They shall no more, land on this shore.
11 They'l single be, so dye I see.
12 They shall be found, both safe & sound
13 Fate do render, one that's tender.

Fig. 242.

Each card bears a name, *Pharoah, Wat Tyler, Mahomett, Semiramis, Fryer Bacon, Dr. Dee, Dido, Herod, Merlin, Dr. Faustus and Prosperina, the daughter of Jupiter.*

The finishing sentence on this instruction card reads :—

"The stars fortell, they love you well. Sold by John Lenthall,' Stationer at the Talbot against St. Dunsden Church, Fleet Street, London.'

Rowley & Co. 1790.

An English pack brought out in 1790 by Rowley & Co. has for the four suits Clubs, represented by a green three-leaved clover; Diamonds showing a red diamond with eight smaller ones upon it; Spades, represented by the short spata flat-sided sword; and Hearts by a red chalice with a dark red heart engraved upon it.

The Court cards, upon which are figures in the dress of the period, are probably intended for portraits.

Fig. 243. George III. King of Hearts.

HEARTS (CHALICE).

The King.	George III, King of England. Fig. 243.
The Queen.	Queen Charlotte.
The Knave.	Beefeater, with badge of Crown on his chest.

DIAMONDS.

The King.	King of Spain, Charles IV.
The Queen.	Queen of Spain.
The Knave.	Soldier wearing conical hat and holding partizan.

CLUBS (Green Clover leaf).

The King	King of Prussia, Frederick William II.
The Queen.	Queen of Prussia. Fig. 244.
The Knave.	Soldier with a double eagle on his cap.

SPADES (Short Sword).

The King.	Louis XVI, King of France. Fig. 245.
The Queen.	Queen of France.
The Knave.	Soldier with wig and pigtail, holding a lance.

Fig. 244. Queen of Prussia. Fig. 245. Louis XVI. King of France.

The Ace of Diamonds (red) has a large diamond in an oval frame of oak leaves, with nine other diamonds engraved upon it, surmounted with the caduceus, the trident and the winged hat of Mercury.

The Ace of Spades (black) shows a short dagger or sword in the oval, bearing the motto *"Honi soit qui mal y pense,"* and surmounted with a large crown and the wording "Geo. III Rex. No. 14." *"Dieu et mon droit,"* Rowley & Co. This card is the "duty-card."

The Ace of Clubs (green) shows the three-leaved clover (trifolium) in an oval frame with various agricultural implements.

The Ace of Hearts (red) shows a chalice with a dark red heart engraved upon it, in a framework of olive leaves and fruit, the whole being surmounted by a bishop's mitre with a cross and bishop's staff.

All the cards are printed from engraved copper plates.

Baker & Co., 1813.

A pack of nicely designed and coloured cards entitled "Eclectic Cards," was published in 1813 by Baker & Co. They were advertised in a pamphlet which accompanied them as "A short account of Baker & Co.'s Complete, Grand, Historical, Eclectic Cards, for England, Ireland, Scotland and Wales; being a selection or an Eclectic Company of Twelve of the most eminent Personages that ever distinguished themselves in those respective Countries, for Heroic deeds, Wisdom, etc;" and the other forty Cards are descriptive of the Local and National Emblems of the Four Nations.

> Historian, Poet, Painter all combine,
> To charm the eye, the taste and mind refine;
> Fancy and sentiment their aid impart,
> To raise the genius, and to mend the heart.

He gives the price as follows:—

> "Price, third class, 15*s.*; second class, 17*s.* 6d.; first class, 20*s*. London. Printed by Theodore Page, Blackfriars Road. 1813."

Then follows the dedication which commences thus:—"*With most humble submission to* every respectable person in the British Empire," and after this a lengthy description and the twelve-page pamphlet concludes as follows:—

> "In the selection which we have made to form our set of court-cards, we have, as we before observed, chosen them from among those characters who have rendered themselves most conspicuous in the history of the United Kingdom. In this particular we have had recourse not only to historical truth, which we have rigidly observed, but we have taken care to fix upon personages who lived at different periods, and which are calculated in colour, variety of dress, and characteristic features, to form an agreeable and elegant contrast, and to avoid that

unpleasant monotony which must have taken place if they had all been selected from the same period of time, and it will be a peculiar gratification to us in our attempts to form a set of cards should we contribute in the smallest degree to augment the elegant and rational amusement of taste and fashion."

Fig. 246.

Fig. 247.

The size of the "Eclectic Cards" is $4\frac{5}{8}$ inches by $2\frac{7}{8}$ inches, nearly 1 inch longer than the ordinary modern cards. The signs of the four suits are: Acorns for England instead of Clubs; red Hearts for Ireland; yellow Diamonds for Scotland; black heavy two-edged Swords for Wales, instead of Spades, called the Spate as used by the Ancient Britons.

The pamphlet gives the following description of the Court cards:

FOR ENGLAND.

KING OF ACORNS.	Arthur, the great and Victorious Hero, King of Britain.
QUEEN OF ACORNS.	Elizabeth, the Wise and Virtuous Queen of England. See fig. 246.
KNIGHT OF ACORNS.	Sir John Falstaff, Knight of England, and companion of Henry V. Fig. 3.

FOR IRELAND.

KING OF HEARTS.	Gathelus, the Grecian prince, King of Ireland.
QUEEN OF HEARTS.	Scotia, his wife, the Egyptian Princess, Queen of Ireland.
KNIGHT OF HEARTS.	Ossian, the Warrior and Poet, Son of Fingal, Knight of Ireland.

FOR SCOTLAND.

KING OF DIAMONDS.	Achaius, King of Scots.
QUEEN OF DIAMONDS.	Mary Stuart, the unfortunate Dowager Queen of France and Queen of Scots.
KNIGHT OF DIAMONDS.	Merlin, the Magic Prophet, the father of King Arthur, Uter Pendragon, etc.

FOR WALES.

KING OF SPATA.	Camber, the third son of Brute, King of Cambria.
QUEEN OF SPATA.	Elfrida, the beautiful Queen of Mona.
KNIGHT OF SPATA.	Thaliessin, the Welch Bard and Poet, etc.

"And as we have now restored that most ancient and most honourable order of the Knights of the Round Table, under its great patron and founder Prince Arthur of immortal memory, the great champion for chivalry, religion, and liberty, the Briton's king and emperor, we here insert a list of this our first installation, with a brief account of their history, and cause of selection."

There is a great deal more in the same strain and Messrs. Baker & Co. were evidently very proud of their production of this pack.

On the left-hand side of the cards 1 to 10 is a long spray of laurel leaves, and on the right side of each suit is a spray representative of the country, viz.:—Oak leaves for England, Shamrock for Ireland, Thistles for Scotland and Leeks for Wales.

The four of Hearts, Fig. 247 shows the spray of Shamrock on the right hand side of the card.

Proverbs, cir. 1780.

This pack consists of various proverbs with quaint line drawing illustrating them. On 9 of Hearts the proverb *"It's an Ill winde Blowes Noebody Good"* is illustrated by two men, one of whom has opened his coat. In doing so he has lost some coins from a bag of money he is carrying, and these are being picked up by people behind him. Fig. 248.

Fig. 248. Fig. 249.

The King of Diamonds has on it, "*If you'l avoid old Charon the fferry man, consult Dr. Dyett, Dr. Quiett and Dr. Merryman,*" and this is illustrated by three sedate old men in long robes. Fig. 249.

"*Look before you leap,*" is on the Ace of Hearts; "*An ounce of mirth is worth a pound of sorrow*" on the nine of Spades; while the Queen of Hearts has the proverb "*Many hands make quick work*"; and the Knave of Spades, "*All is grist that comes to the mill.*"

On the 4 of Spades is "*Halfe an houres hanging hinder Three Miles Rideing,*" and this shows a man who has hanged himself while his horse is waiting near by.

Fig. 250.

Fig. 251.

On the eight of Diamonds the illustration shows a number of women and geese, all mixed up in a quarrel and the wording "*Where there are women and geese there wants noe noise.*"

The five of Clubs shows a woman who has come to a house to search for her daughter, whom she finds concealed in a cupboard, with a man's hat and coat lying close by. The proverb reads "*The old woman had never look'd in the oven for her Daughter had she not been there herselfe,*" Fig. 251. On the eight of Spades, Fig. 250, "*Two of a Trade can never Agree.*"

On each of the numeral cards the sign of the suit is printed on the right hand top corner, and the value of the card in Roman figures on the left, but on the King, Queen and Knave the titles are at the top of the card in the centre. Some of the cards are rather gross and repulsive and most of the illustrations are poor in design and execution. They date from about 1780.

Aesop's Fables.

Another interesting pack, which may be classed under the heading of "Moral Cards," is one on which cleverly executed woodcuts are printed representing on each of the fifty-two cards one of Aesop's Fables. The suit signs and values are shown as miniature cards at the top left-hand corner. The title of the fable is over the picture, and underneath are four lines of rhyme giving particulars of the story: the whole being summed up and condensed into the "moral" at the bottom of the card, which consists of two lines of good advice, very much to the point.

Fig. 252 illustrate the fable entitled "The Old Man and Death."

Fig. 252.

Fig. 253.

On page 167 the fable of the "Dog and Ox" is seen on the three of Diamonds, where the dog is lying in the manger and snarling at the ox who requests to have the food which the dog cannot himself eat. Fig 254.

MORAL.

"Sordid ill nature thus doth oft Refuse,
To give to Others what it Cannot use."

Fig. 254.

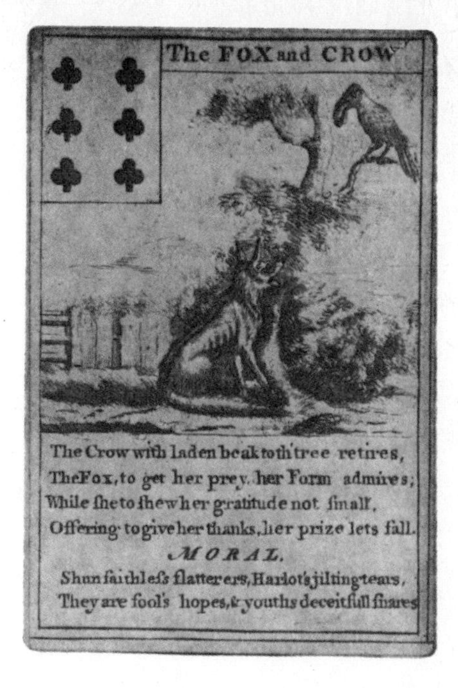

Fig. 255.

Fig. 256.

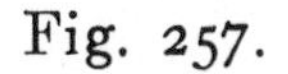
Fig. 257.

On the Knave of Clubs, Fig. 257, the fable of the "Fox and Stork" is illustrated, showing the stork with her long beak enjoying the dinner which she has placed in a "glass violl," whilst the Fox can only look on.

MORAL.

"Fraud is by fraud but justly paid again,
And to deceive the Cozner is no Shame."

The fable on the six of Clubs is the well-known one of the "Fox and the Crow," the moral reading :—

"Shun faithless flatterers, Harlot's jilting tears,
They are fool's hopes and youth's deceitfull snares." Fig. 255.

On the Knave of Hearts we see the Crane extracting the bone from the throat of the Wolf. Asking the Wolf for payment she is told "Fond fool, go thank me for thy head," the moral reading :—

"Well meaning Love is often paid with Hate,
And a good nature's lost on an Ingrate." Fig. 256.

On the King of Clubs the fable of the "Lyon and Mouse" is given and is the sequel to the familiar one where the mouse releases the lion from his entanglement in the snare, which fable is illustrated on the King of Spades. This engraving shows the mouse being accidentally crushed under the paw of the lion's daughter, whôm he demands in marriage.

"The mouse for his late Service fill'd with pride,
Demands the Royal Virgin for his bride,
The match agreed he in flame admired
He unawares crush'd by her Paw expir'd."

MORAL.

"Ill judg'd Ambishion oft itself Destroys,
And what it hopes for most it least enjoys."

Two of Clubs, Fig. 253, illustrates the Eagle and Tortoise.

The designs on each of the fifty-two cards are very clever drawings and were probably executed by Kirk, whose signature is on many of them.

POLITICAL. Titus Oates Plot.

In 1679 there was published a newspaper called "*True Domestick Intelligence,*" and in No. 35 for November 4th of that year is an advertisement as follows :—

> " The Horrid Popish Plot lively represented in a Pack of Cards Printed for Jonathan Wilkins and Jacob Sampson."

In No. 50 of the " True Domestick Intelligence" for December 26, 1679, occurs this advertisement :—

> " There is lately published a new Pack of Cards neatly cut in copper, in which are represented to the life the several consults for killing the King and extirpating the Protestant Religion, the manner of the murthering Sir Edmondbury Godfrey, the Tryals and Executions of the Conspirators, and all other material designs relating to the contrivance and management of the said horrid Popish Plot, with their attempt to throw it on the Protestants. These have something more than the first have, and yet nothing left out that was in them nor any old impertinent things added. Printed and sold by Robert Walton at the Globe, on the north side of St. Paul's Churchyard, near the West end, where you may have a pack for eightpence of the very best, you may have them in sheets fit to adorn studies and houses. There is likewise a broadside with an almanack, and some of the aforesaid pictures about it, which may not unfitly be called the Christian Almanack fit for Shops, Houses and Studies. Sold as above said, the price Sixpence."

In my collection I have the two packs referred to in these two advertisements, and although the illustrations on both packs represent the same episodes connected with this plot, the positions of the figures in the pictures are reversed from left to right, the suit signs and values are also in different positions, but the descriptive wording is the same in both packs, and there seems little doubt that one pack has been copied from the other by reflection, which would explain the reversed position.

The packs consist of 52 Cards, bearing the usual suit sign with Roman figures showing the value, and as explained in the advertisement, "represents to the life the several consults for killing the King, &c," and the various incidents in what is generally known as "The Titus Oates Plot." Four of these cards are illustrated and here are some of the titles from the cards :—

The Ace of Hearts shows the Pope, who is holding a key, three Cardinals and a Bishop seated at a table, beneath which the devil is seen crouching. The wording reads :—

"*The plot first hatcht at Rome, by the Pope and Cardinalls.*" ......

On the six of Clubs Fig. 258, "*Capt. Berry and Alderman Brooks are offerd £500 to cast the Plot on the Protestants.*"

On the five of Clubs, Fig. 259, "*The Execution of the 5 Iesuitts.*"

On Knave of Diamonds, Fig. 260, "*Pickerin attempts to kill ye K. in St. Iames' Park.*" Pickering is crouching behind a tree while the King passes with his attendants, who are wearing very large wigs.

On the six of Hearts, Fig. 261, "*Coleman drawn to his execution.*" Coleman seems to be rather enjoying his ride.

On the three of Clubs the picture shows two men talking to a servant girl with the wording: "*Gifford and Stubbe give money to a maid to fire her Master's House*" and on the three of the same suit is shown a great fire in progress with people carrying goods in sacks and chests with the wording.

London Remember 2nd September 1666.

Fig. 258.

Fig. 259.

Five of the series represents capital punishments, and five others have particulars of corruptions.

On the three and six of Clubs.

On the Queen of Clubs, "*Redding endeavouring to corrupt Capt. Bedloe.*"

On the four of Hearts' "*Coleman giveth a Guiny to Incourage ye four Ruffians.*"

On the three of Diamonds, "*Ashby received instruction of Whitebread for the Society to offer Sr. George Wakeman* £10,000" [to poison the King.]

The whole story as told on this pack of cards shows the display of popular feeling, while the publication of such a partizan character points out in a remarkable way the agitated state of the public mind, while under the untruthful revelations of Titus Oates, Bedloe and others.

The cards of this pack are printed from engraved copper plates, and a number of other packs in the same style were engraved about this time relating to various political happenings.

Fig. 260.

Fig. 261.

Spanish Armada, cir. 1590.

A pack published after the defeat of the Spanish Armada illustrates the chief events connected there-with.

This famous armament consisting of 150 ships, 2650 great guns, 30,000 soldiers and sailors, arrived in the English Channel on July 19th, 1588, and was defeated by Drake and Howard, who maintained a running fight from July 21st to 27th, forcing the shattered fleet to bear away for Scotland and Ireland, where a storm dispersed most of them, the remainder returning to Spain by way of the North Sea.

Fig. 262.

Fig. 263.

On the pack mentioned above the values and suit signs are placed at the top of each card and the remainder of the space is taken up by a copper plate engraving with some quaint wording underneath. Two of these cards are shown. On the Queen of Clubs, Fig. 262, we see the Pope, wearing his triple crown and standing near a table on which are three bags of money. His right hand is placed on the head of one of three men, as if in the act of blessing, and it would appear that the Pope is about to hand over this money to aid Spain in her attempt against England. The wording runs :—"*The pope gives a million of gold to help the Spaniard.*" On the KING OF CLUBS, Fig. 263, Queen Elizabeth is seen consulting with some of her Admirals. She is wearing her crown and holds her sceptre in her right hand, and in the background the masts of a number of ships can be seen. The wording below reads :— "*Q. Elizabeth prepares a strong fleet, Ld. Howard, Ld. Seymour, Sr. Francis Drake, Commanders.*"

On the TWO OF CLUBS :—"*King of Spain consults the enlarging his Empire by the Conquest of England.*"

On the Ace of Clubs :—"*The Pope and Traiterous English fugitives consult the Conquest of England.*"

On the NINE OF HEARTS are represented "*The twelve Spanish Shipps caled the* 12 *Apostles.*"

On the EIGHT OF CLUBS "*The third fight between ye Eng'h and Spanish Fleetes, being the 25th of June* 1588, *where in ye English had again ye better.*"

The SEVEN OF SPADES shows the "*Spanish ships castaway on the Irish Shoare with marriners and seaman.*"

On the THREE OF SPADES we have "*Queen Eliz: with Nobles and Gentry and a great number of people giving God humble thanks in St. Paul's church and having set upp the Ensigns taken from the Spaniards.*"

This interesting pacfl of cards (which are uncoloured) are printed from engraved copper plates, and the two illustrations, show exact copies of the original cards.

Rump Parliament, cir. 1684.

A pack of fifty-two cards illustrating various episodes relating to the Commonwealth, was probably produced in Holland during the residence in that country of Charles II. They are of a satirical nature and refer to the public and private actions and conduct of Oliver Cromwell and various members of the so-called Rump Parliament.

They are printed from engraved copper plates and each picture is well drawn and full of artistic merit, with a description of each subject under.

Fig. 264. Fig. 265.

The TEN OF HEARTS, Fig. 265, shows a number of men seated in a large barrel, while others are being pushed out through an opening at the top; with this wording :—

"The Rump and dreggs of the house of Com. remaining after the good members were purged out."

The TEN OF SPADES, Fig. 264, shows Oliver Cromwell and his companions praying, which is explained as follows :—

"Oliver seaking God while the K. is murthered by his order."

FOUR OF HEARTS. A number of men round a fire, one of whom is throwing salt over some joint hanging on a gibbet —

"The Rump roasted, salt it well, it stinks exceedingly."

ACE OF CLUBS shows a man assaulting a lady, while others are committing robbery, &c. :—

"A Free State, or a toleration of all sort of villany."

KING OF CLUBS. Oliver Cromwell is seen with hands raised in benediction, standing among a group of his followers :—

"Oliver declares himself and the Rebells to be the Godly Party."

QUEEN OF SPADES. Oliver is seen with his arms around a lady's waist, with this explanation :—

"The Lady Lambert and Oliver under a Strong Conflict."

Only three perfect packs are known, and only one of these has the extra card, bearing in an oval the title "The Knavery of the RUMP Lively represented in a Pack of Cards." At the top of the oval are two figures, one representing the Devil, and the other Oliver Cromwell, and a scroll issuing from his mouth reads :—*"Set us accord for a good old cause."* At the bottom :—*"To be sold by* R. T. *near Stationers hall, and at the black Bull in Cornhill."*

Note from Auctioneer's Catalogue respecting these cards :—

"This pack is the most elaborately engraved of all the sets o English pictorial cards, and complete packs are very rare."

Duke of Monmouth, cir. 1685

A pictoriai pack of cards was published soon after the death of Charles II, illustrating the various incidents which took place during the rebellion raised by the Duke of Monmouth, the natural son of Charles II by Lucy Waters. He was banished from England in 1683 for his connection with the Rye House Plot. He invaded England at Lyme, June 11th, 1685, and was proclaimed King at Taunton on June 20th, but was defeated at Sedgmoor on July 6th and beheaded on Tower Hill, on July 15th.

Fig. 266. Fig. 267.

On the Knave of Clubs a man is shown standing upon a drum with the title :—

> "*Ferguson Preaching to the Rebells ye day before ye defeat on Iosh.* 22, *v.* 22."

On the six of Clubs "*The Late D. of M. entering Lime with* 1500 *Men.*"

On the KING OF SPADES Fig. 266, we see a man who appears to be much frightened at the sight of two very ugly winged devils, flying over his head, and in the background the whole army is shown in flight. The title at the bottom of the card reads: "*Devills in ye Ayre Bewitching Ms. Army.*"

On the six of Spades "*The late D. of M: Ld. Grey & a German carried to ye Tower.*"

On the seven of Spades "*The late D. of M. beheaded on Tower Hill 15 July 1685.*"

The title on the Queen of Spades, Fig. 267 is:—"*The late D. of Ms. Standard,*" and a large flag is displayed with the wording upon it "FEAR NOTHING BUT GOD."

On the Queen of Diamonds a Number of women are kneeling before Monmouth:—

"*The Gogly Maids o Taunton presenting their Colours upon their knees to the D. of M.*"

On the three of Hearts "*Argyle Executed and his head affixed on ye TALLBOOTH.*"

The date 1685 appears on the eight of Hearts with the wording "*Bonfires made the 26th of Iuly att night being the thanksgiving for the victory: —1685.*"

James II, cir. 1688.

A pictorial political pack published about 1688 illustrates the sequence of events during the reign of King James II, 1685-1688. The major part of each card is occupied by an illustration, a description of which fills the portion below it. At the top is the suit mark on the right, and the value is indicated by Roman numbers on the left. The designs on the cards are from copper plates, rather badly executed, and uncoloured.

Some of the inscriptions, which are often very badly spelt, are as follows:—

ACE OF HEARTS—"The King leaving London about three o'clock in the morning in his barge."

5 OF HEARTS—"The Chancellor going to the Tower and is followed by many more of the Brethren."

9 of Hearts—"The Earle of Essex is Murdered in the Tower."

8 of Hearts—"A Raysor is seen thrown out at window in the Tower where the Earle of Essex was." Fig. 268.

7 of Hearts—"The Prince of Orange coming to St. Iameses is received with great Joy." Fig. 269.

Fig. 268.

Fig. 269.

3 of Spades—"The Duchess of Modena Presenting a wedge of gold to Lady of Loreta that ye Q might conceive a Son."

6 of Spades—"Many of ye Nobility of England in Councill about ye Dainger of England."

7 of Spades—"Sum of ye Nobility of England are sending their Memorialls of their distress to ye Prince of Oring."

9 of Spades—"The Prince and Princes of Oring Receve the Memoriall and Inuitasion from England."

Ace of Diamonds—"Many witnesses sworn before a great body of ye Peers that ye child was a Lawfull Prince of Wales."

KING OF HEARTS—"The ould Oxford Regiment of Horse with 2 more first left the King and went to the Prince."

QUEEN OF HEARTS—"A fight at Reding wherein the Irish Souldiers suffered most, the people fireing out at window on them." Fig. 270.

KNAVE OF HEARTS—"The Queen and Child and father Peters going away in the night."

ACE OF SPADES—"500 Thousand pounds sent from France yearly to Charles the 2 to keep the sitting of Parliament of."

Fig. 270.

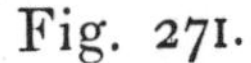

Fig. 271.

2 OF DIAMONDS—"The Queen is brought to bed of a boy." "Reported so." Fig. 270.

9 OF DIAMONDS—"The yong Child going to Portsmouth garded by ye Lord Sallsbereys Trups of Papists."

4 OF CLUBS—"About 200 Ministers suspended in ye Cunuey of Duram for not reading the Kings Declaration."

6 OF CLUBS—"The Bishops are Sent to the Tower by Watter."

7 OF CLUBS—"The Bishops are cleared at theyr triall, 2 of ye Judges were displaced after they giving for the Bishops."

Taken altogether these fifty-two cards give the story of the abdication of James and the Coming of William and Mary.

James II, cir. 1689.

Another pack illustrates events which took place during the later part of the reign of James II. It portrays the landing of the Prince of Orange and episodes connected with the attempts to restore Roman Catholicism in England. The designs are fairly good, and the cards are printed from engraved metal plates and are uncoloured.

The suit and value marks are at the top of each card, with an Arabic numeral which indicates its place in the sequence of events.

Fig. 272. Fig. 273.

The three of Clubs Fig. 272, shows a man tied to the tail of a cart and the title below says :—

*"Oates Whipt from Algate to Tyburn."**

On the Queen of Clubs we have a rather gruesome scene depicting a women in the act of cutting off a man's leg with a large chopper.

* Titus Oates, etc, page 169.

The wording gives the following explanation :—

"The Midwife cutting her Husband to Pieces." Fig. 273.

Other titles are :—

7 of Clubs.	*"The Tryal of the Seaven Bishops."*
9 of Clubs.	*"The Seaven Bisshops goin to the Tower."* Fig. 274.
Ace of Clubs.	*"The Earle of Essex's throat cut."*
2 of Spades.	*"The popish Midwife burning."*

Fig. 274. Fig. 275.

5 of Spades.	*"Doing of Penance up a high hill with Peas in his Shoes."*
Queen of Spades.	*"Madam W———ks at Confession."*
5 of Diamonds.	*"The prince of Orange coming to London."*
7 of Diamonds.	*"The Fight at Redding."*
9 of Diamonds.	*"The Prince of Orange landing."* Fig. 275.
Ace of Hearts.	*"My Lord Chancellor in the Tower."*
7 of Hearts.	*"A Priest selling of Relicks by Auction."*
10 of Hearts.	*"The Army going over to ye Prince of Orange."*
King of Hearts.	*"My Ld. Mayor and Sheriffs wait on ye Prince at Windsor."*

This pack is one of a number of political packs published during the reigns of Charles II and James II. They were generally of a satirical character and some of the cards were rather vulgar.

Duke of Marlborough cir. 1705.

This pack illustrates the battles and victories of the Duke of Marlborough, and also various happenings during the dispute as to the Spanish Succession, or the House of Hanover.

A number of the Coat cards have portraits of the illustrious persons taking part in, or connected with the dispute, while the thirteen cards of the Suit of Spades are a series of severe satire on Louis XIV.

Fig. 276.

Fig. 277.

On the King of Spades a man is shown who is carrying a crown, while some men behind him shout: *"Stop Thief,"* and the wording on the card reads :—

"All Europ's Riveted in this Belief,
My Grandfather before me was a Thief.
I'll steal Spain's Crown and Jewels with its pelf
And be at last a Nominal King my self."

Three of Spades. A young man holds up a crown in his left hand, and in his right he carries an auctioneer's hammer. In front of him are four ecclesiastics (one of whom is the Pope) and he asks "*Who bids most*" to which question the Pope replies "*The Kingdom of Jerusalem.*"

The wording at bottom :—
The Royal Outcry, or ye Dauphine selling by Auction ye reversion of his Father's Crown.

The four of Spades shows the King on his death-bed, two women are near, one of whom offers him a cup, and the wording under reads "*Give Him Blood to Drink.*"

On the seven of Spades :—
"*Thus all my Spongey Officers I serve*
Squeeze out their ill got Wealth and let 'em starve."

On the Knave of Hearts, Fig. 276, a man is sitting at a grid with bags of money upon it, some of which is seen falling through, and another is saying to him "*Oh Rogue,*" to which he replies : "*I am not the first.*" At the foot are the words :—
"*Had you my Post, pray would not you tell mony over as I do*"

The portraits on some of the Coat cards are :—

King of Hearts	George, Prince of Denmark, Born 1653.
Queen of Hearts	ANNA Sophia of Hannover, Born 1630. Fig. 277
King of Diamonds	Victor, Duke of Saxony, Born 1663.
Queen of Diamonds	Princess Royal of Prussia.
King of Clubs	Charles III, King of Spain, Born Oct. 1, 1685,
Queen of Clubs	Anne, by ye Grace of God of Great Britain. France and Ireland. Queen Defender of ye Faith.
Ten of Clubs	Prince Eugene of Savoy, Born Oct. 18, 1663.

Many of the cards show the various battles both on sea and land, and the whole is one of the best engraved of the many pictorial packs that were published at this period.

South Sea Bubble, cir. 1720.

A Scheme for paying-off the National Debts of France was established in 1710 by John Law of Edinburgh (later called Law's Bubble)* the capital of which is said to have amounted to £100,000,000, and when it burst in 1720, was the ruin of thousands of people. In the same year, 1710, the South Sea Company (afterwards known as the South Sea Bubble) was started in England. This company was first unwisely and later dishonestly managed, and came to grief in 1720 ruining thousands of families.

Fig. 278. Fig. 279.

Almost all the wealthy persons in the kingdom had become speculators and the shares, originally £100, rose to £1,000. A parliamentary inquiry took place in November 1720, and Aislabie, Chancellor of the Exchequer, and several Members of Parliament were expelled from the House and the Director's estates, to the value of £2,014,000 were seized and sold in 1721. Knight, the cashier, absconded with £100,000, but later he compounded the fraud for £10,000 and returned to England in 1743.

* Page 128.

After the bursting of the Bubble Companies a pack of 52 cards was issued, suggesting in a sarcastic manner, the turning of various trades and professions into companies. At the top the name of a trade is printed, and a small replica of a playing card shown. Beneath are illustrations of the trade, with four lines of doggerel verse, a few of which are here given :—

The six of Spades, Fig. 278, shows an Insurance Office, with the title "INSURANCE ON LIVES" explained by the wording,

> Come all ye Generous Husbands, with your Wives,
> Insure round sums on your precarious Lives :—
> That to your comfort, when you're Dead & Rotten,
> Your Widows may be Rich when you're forgotten.

The Knave of Clubs, Fig. 279, "THE FREEHOLDER," invites "Ye Spendthrift Prodigals" to sell their land and invest in South Sea Stock.

> Come all ye Spendthrift Prodigals, that hold
> Free Land and want to turn the Same to Gold
> We'll Buy your all, provided you'll agree
> To drown your Purchase Money in South Sea.

Fig. 280.

The illustration on the Queen of Diamonds, Fig. 280, entitled "FURNISHING OF FUNERALS" shows a funeral procession,

On the King of Hearts entitled "WHALE FISHERY" is shown a very large whale with three small boats, one of which has been capsized.

There is an extra card, without any suit signs, showing a female figure at the top holding a scroll with the wording :—

"Stock Jobbing Cards, or the Humours of Change Alley." Under this is a busy scene in a street crowded with people, horses, &c., and probably intended to show the sale of bogus shares. At the bottom of the card is printed :—

Think with what haste Unthinking Fools are Running
To Humour Knaves and Gratify their Cunning ;
All seemed Transported with Joyfull Madness,
But soon their mighty Hopes will turn to Sadness.

Fig. 281.

Fig. 282.

Love Mottoes, cir. 1720.

A pack of fifty-two cards published about 1720 are mostly of a satirical character, each card having a clever illustration (in mezzotint) with the explanation in rhyme below. At the top left-hand corner is a representation of a small playing-card, and the suits are the ordinary ones of Diamonds, Hearts, Clubs and Spades.

On the Knave of Spades Fig. 281, we see a faun dancing with a young girl, and below is a couplet :—

"We'll merrily dance and sportfully play,
And kiss the tedious hours away."

On the three of Diamonds Fig. 282, is a clever print of two cupids at play, or at mischief. They are turning over a large basket of fruit, which would appear to belong to Venus, as we read below :—

"Venus no more will trust her giddy Boy
To fetch her fruit when he's so full of ioy."

On the four of Spades Cupid is peacefully sleeping, while a nymph has taken his bow and is breaking it across her knee. The accompanying lines are below :—

"The nymphs no more will fear thy dreadful bow
'tis broken now and all thy arrows too."

On the Queen of Diamonds a lady is singing and playing on a harpsichord, and a gentleman is saying to her :—

"Oh Cytherea, take the fatall choice,
or veil your Beauty, or Supress your Voice."

The Knave of Clubs shows a man seated at a table upon which are a number of cards. He has evidently manipulated one, to the great surprise of his victim, who is handing him some money.

High pas, begone, the silver disappears,
The Juglar laughs, the Gull does scratch his ears."

The six of Hearts shows a gentleman who is kissing a lady's hand, with the following couplet :—

"Madam, I am your Slave, the Coxcomb cryes,
Ten thousand Cupids revell in your eyes."

The above will give some idea of the love-sick rhymes which are found on most of these cards.

Scotch Heraldic, cir. 1690

A pack of 54 Heraldic cards was published about 1690 bearing the arms of England, Ireland, Scotland and France together with those of Lords, Viscounts, and Earls. The suit signs are the usual Spades, Hearts Clubs and Diamonds, and the Honour Cards are King, Queen, and Prince. The arms on the Kings and Queens are as follows :—

SUIT.	KINGS.	QUEENS.
Spades..................	Arms of France.	Duke of Gordon.
Hearts..................	Arms of Scotland.	Duke of Hamilton.
Clubs....................	Arms of England.	Duke of Lennox.
Diamonds..............	Arms of Ireland.	Duke of Queensberry.

Fig. 283.

Fig. 284.

One of the four Princes, Fig. 283, bears the arms of Graham, Marquess of Montrose.
The 10, 9, 8, 7 and 6 of each suit bear the arms of Earls.
The 5 and 4 „ „ „ Viscounts.
The 3, 2 and Ace „ „ „ Lords.

A supplementary card illustrates "*The Town of Edingburh Armes*" another "*The Seale of the Lyon Office Impaled with the Armes of Sir Alexander Arieskn*—present Lyon, King of Armes.*" These two cards have no suit marks or values.

The four of Clubs (Viscounts) has three shields showing the arms of Drummond, Graham, and Dalrymple. Fig. 284.

These cards were engraved by Walter Scott, a goldsmith of Edinburgh, and give the arms as they existed about 1690. Sir Walter Scott possessed one of these packs at Abbotsford, and has made a note about the engraver, "one Walter Scott, goldsmith of Edinburgh, was admitted into the fraternity of his craft in 1686 and another Walter in 1701."

A complete pack was lent by Miss Crichton to the Heraldic Exhibition held at Edinburgh in 1891, and the fifty-four cards are illustrated in the Catalogue of the Exhibition.

* This pack was engraved by Walter Scott, the Edinburgh Goldsmith, and prepared under the direction of the Lyon King of Arms, Sir Alexander Erskine.

English Heraldic, cir. 1686.

An Heraldic Pack issued about 1686 has the usual suit signs marked at the top of the card on the left and the value of the card in Roman figures on the right for the numerals and K for King, Q for Queen and P for Prince (Knave).

This pack, which consists of the arms of the English nobility displayed on the various cards seems to correspond with a pack advertised by John Dugdale, London, 1684, and it is thought the composition of the heraldry was the work of Gregory King, Somerset Herald, his name being mentioned in *Watt's Bibliotheca Britannica,* in connection with the issuing of "*A pack of Cards containing the Arms of the English Nobility, London,* 1684."

The arms which are emblazoned under the various titles of Dukes, Viscounts, Barons and Earles are numbered, probably agreeing with a printed list, but the arms of the Bishops are not numbered. Fig. 286.

In the issue of the "*Observator*" of February 1686 there is an advertisement of a pack as follows :—"*Cards containing the arms of the King and all Lords, Spiritual and Temporal, of England,*" sold by E. Evets at the Green Dragon, St. Paul's Churchyard."

Two years later another pack was brought out with various additions and alterations. For instance, in the original pack on the Queen of Clubs (Dukes) a blank shield is shown and in the later pack this is filled with the arms of FitzJames, a natural son of James II, who was

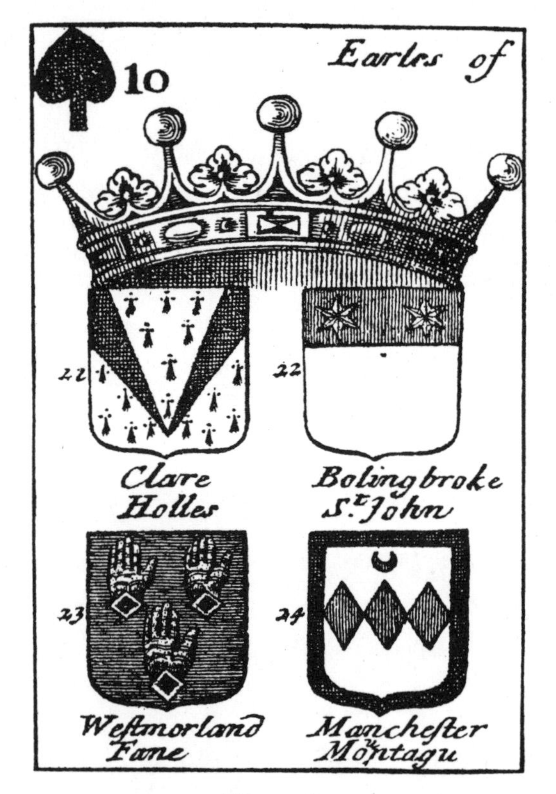

Fig. 285.

made a Duke in 1687, but the opposite happens on the Eight of Clubs (Earles), where the shield with the arms of the Earl of Macclesfield, which appear on the 1684 pack, is shown blank on the later issue, the reason being that he was a personal friend of the Duke of Monmouth, and his name appeared in a list of persons supposed to be against the King. He (very wisely) retired to Holland, but later returned to England with the Prince of Orange, Fig. 275, who appointed him a Privy Councillor.

KING OF HEARTS shows under a large crown the arms of England and Scotland.

On Fig. 285, TEN OF SPADES are the arms of Holles, St. John, Fane and Mountagu.

On Fig. 286, FIVE OF DIAMONDS, under a mitre, are the arms of the Bishops of Bristol, Rochester, Bath and Wells, and Chichester.

On Fig. 287, THE PRINCE OF CLUBS, we have the arms of Clinton, Howard, Sackville, and Cecil.

Fig. 286. Fig. 287.

Chatto, page 132, gives particulars of a wrapper probably belonging to these cards which is in the Bagford's Collection at the British Museum from which it would appear that the publication of these Heraldic Cards was licensed by the Duke of Norfolk, as Earl Marshal of England, and as such entitled to take cognizance of all matters relating to Heraldry.

Musical Cards.

Among the many ideas adopted on cards for educational purposes, music has not been forgotten, and a number of packs have been printed with various musical selections. One pack published about 1730 gives part of John Gay's "Beggars' Opera," which was a satirical attack on Horace Walpole's government.

Fig. 288. Fig. 289.

Figures 288 and 289 show the Ace of Clubs and Knave of Clubs from a pack published by Joseph Galler at Brussells about 1780. The music on these cards is written for the various instruments as marked, and are part of a pack of 42 cards from the collection of Lady Charlotte Schreiber.

On the Queen of Clubs, Fig. 290, we have a later example, from a French pack, about 1820, with the music of a lively waltz.

In the collection at the British Museum there is a pack of Musical Playing Cards, most of them having four lines of music, with the words of a song under each line, followed by four lines of another verse. Under this verse there are two more lines of music, arranged as an accompaniment for the flute. A few have eight lines of music with the words of the song under them. At the upper left-hand corner is a small representation of an ordinary playing card.

Fig. 290.

The Knave of Diamonds is shown as Jack Shephard and we learn that

" The People lament, alack and alack,
'Twas pity to hang up their Favourite Jack ;
For Britains hate thinking, and all would be dumb,
But for Shephard and Faux, Faustus, Wild, and Tom Thumb."

The King of Diamonds, assures his beloved that

" Not all the Diamonds, all the gold
That all the Mines on Earth can hold,
Should tempt me to resign my right
To thee my Diamond, my Delight."

The King of Spades contains the music and words of "The First King."

" When Adam was the King of Spades,
And Eve his wife did sew ;
Then delving was the best of Trades,
No pride no Fraud they knew."

Here are a few of the titles on some of the pip cards. "No fault in loving," "Faithful Love," "Cupid's Snare," "Jovial Toper," "Broken Heart," "Young Damon," and the "True Lover," who concludes as follows :—

" I'll hast to some far distant shore,
And never, never, never, never think of Woman more."

Fig. 291.

Fig. 292.

On the Knave of Spades, Fig. 291, the song under the title is "The Miser," and the words :—

" A Miser's a Knave un-to himself to starve all tho he rowls in Pelf,
With his own Spade he makes his Grave, and Dies to Gold a wretched Slave."

On the Ace of Spades, Fig. 292, we have a lover's mournful song in A flat, entitled "Fair Ingrate."

"Hither Sexton bring thy Spade,
let me in my Tomb be laid,
Life's a Torment and a Pain,
since the Fair does me disdain.

Come, O Death, with Gloomy Charms,
Lock me in thy Clay-Cold Arms,
When I'm Dead this fair Ingrate,
Surely then will cease to hate—

These cards are printed from engraved copper plates, and the songs seem to have been written for the cards.

Quotations, cir. 1820.

Playing Cards have been applied from time to time to help in the study of various branches of learning, and perhaps the strangest use of all is that of trying to inculcate teaching of a moral (or immoral) character.

In an early 19th century pack the wording and illustrations on the Hearts and Diamonds give a series of what one may call good advice, but the wording and illustrations on the Clubs and Spades are of a most indecent character.

One of these cards, Fig. 293, shows the value "three of hearts" by a miniature card on the left-hand top corner. The title "Riches and Poverty" is enclosed in an oval panel, around which are various articles, clothing, boots, puritan-shaped hat, an overflowing bag of gold, &c., and below this, still further to illustrate the title, we see a coach (with a lady inside) drawn by six horses and on the hill-side a man who is ploughing with two horses, while to illustrate poverty, two or three people are sitting near a large empty pot, and a beggar is seen on the left asking alms.

Fig. 294. The "ten of hearts," with appropriate wording illustrates "Justice."

Fig. 293.

Fig. 294.

Old German, cir. 1440.

In the collection of playing cards in the British Museum there are preserved some cards, *circa.* 1440 which were found pasted in the covers of an old book. These are not cut up into single cards but are in two sheets, one of which is shown in Fig. 295. The suits are acorns, bells and hearts, and no doubt the fourth one was leaves, although it is not on the sheets. The court cards shown are King, Knight, and Knave, but there is no indication of a Queen. In this peculiarity they resemble the old German packs where the court cards are King, Obermann (or superior), and Untermann (or inferior) Officer. Mr. Chatto describes the latter as King, Jack and Jack's man.

Fig. 295.

These cards are supposed to have been executed by means of a stencil, but if so, they would appear to have been touched up by hand, for when a stencil alone is used the joining pieces must always show.

The present writer is of the opinion that they were printed from very rough and crude wood blocks.

Mr. Chatto says* :—"From the costume of the figures on these cards, I am inclined to think they are the production of a Venetian card-maker. A lion, the emblem of St. Mark, the patron saint of Venice, and a distinctive badge of the city, appears in the suit of Bells, and a similar figure with part of a mutilated inscription also occurs on the suit of Acorns."

The illustration, Fig. 295, is one of a number of pages mounted on eight small sheets. It shows a King and a Knave of *Herzen* (Hearts), a King of *Eicheln* (Acorns), and portions of three other cards.

These eight sheets are, from an archæological aspect, a most interesting series and are probably the most ancient playing-cards in the British Museum Cabinet..

* Chatto, page 89.

Old German.
Found in Book Cover.

Probably one of the oldest European packs is the one of forty-eight cards, all of which are illustrated by Singer*, who says, "They may safely be placed among the earliest known specimens."

Reduced reproductions (quarter size) of eight cards of this pack are given in Fig. 296. They are the King and two of Hearts; the Knight and seven of Bells; the Knave (with crossbow) and two of Acorns, and the Knave and seven of Leaves. The cards are coloured red and green, and the Knights are distinguished by the suit signs being placed above them, whilst on the Knaves the signs are below. The size of each card is 3 ins. by 2 ins.

Many of them are almost identical with those shown in Fig. 202 The suits are composed of Hearts (*Herzen*), Bells (*Schellen*), Acorns (*Eicheln*), and Leaves (*Grun*), and may be said to represent four classes of people.

The Bells are such as were usually tied to hawks, and denote the Nobility, who alone would own these birds.**

Hearts represent the Ecclesiastics or the Priesthood, as do the cups or chalices on the Spanish cards.

* Singer, Page 172.

** On the Bayeux Tapestry, Harold carries a hawk upon his wrist as a sign of his noble birth.

The Leaves represent the gentry who own lands, mansions and parks, while the acorns signify the peasants or workers.‡

Each suit is made up of twelve cards, which nine are numerals, and three are coat cards, viz., King, Knight or Oberman, and Knave or Untermann. There are no aces and no queens.

Fig. 296.

On the two of each suit are two crossed mallets—the mark of the printer. In addition, a Unicorn couchant is shown on the two of Acorns, and Dr. Stukeley (who discovered these cards in the covers of an old book) says this was the badge of Richard II and he thinks they may have been made during his reign, which would date them between 1377 and 1399.

‡ Page 74.

Pack on Pieces of Bone.

Made by Prisoners of War.

Part of a rather unique pack of Cards (?) in the author's collection consists of pieces of bone on which the usual suit signs are painted by hand. They were made by prisoners during the Great War 1914-18, who in order to play their favourite game saved the pieces of bone, cut and shaped them into a more or less uniform size, and thus manufactured a useable, if clumsy, pack.

In Fig. 297 eight of these pieces show the exact size of the originals. Each piece is about one-sixteenth of an inch in thickness, scraped and polished smooth on one side, then the Coat cards and numerals painted upon them as near as possible like the ordinary suit signs.

Fig. 297.

The cards illustrated above are:—

The two and nine of Spades.

The two, nine and Queen of Hearts.

The ten of Diamonds.

The four and nine of Clubs.

The King.

There seems little doubt that the representation of the King on our English cards is intended as a portrait of that bluff monarch Henry VIII. This is not merely conjecture, but is supported by the likeness to the many portraits we have of this notorious King, who was described by a school-boy as "a great widower." Fig. 298.

In France the Court cards often bear the names of Royal or celebrated personages, and they were evidently assumed in order to do honour to the Kings, their Queens, or mistresses or other persons who happened to be in favour at the time the particular packs were printed. On very early cards we find Corsube and Apollen.

Fig. 298. Fig. 299.

On a pack dated about 1500 (Louis the Twelfth) are the names of Charles, Sezar (Cæsar), Artus and David. Later, about 1525, after the marriage of Francis I with Eleanor of Spain, the names of the King Cards were changed to Julius Cæsar, Charles, Hector, and David. In successive reigns, also, events at Court were chronicled on the cards, and not only were names altered, but costumes, designs and weapons changed with the period. Later still, in 1590 (Henry the Fourth) we find Carel, Melun, and Capet among the Kings.

During the French Revolution it was not only the members of the Royal family, who were beheaded, but the Kings and Queens of all the suits were banished and names and representations of sages and philosophers such as SOLON, PLATON, CATON and BRUTUS were substituted.

On an Austrian pack the names of the Kings are JEAN I. ER, CHARLES QUINT, BAUDOUIN DE CONSTANTINOPLE and GODEFROID DE BOUILLON.

The Queen.

In the earliest cards used in Italy, Spain, and Germany there was no queen, but in time the Italians introduced her into their packs making four court cards, viz. :—King, Queen, Chevalier and Valet. These, with the forty numerals added to the twenty-two Atouts, made up the pack of seventy-eight which is generally known as the Tarot pack.

Fig. 300. Fig. 301.

England, when she adopted the French cards, introduced a particular queen of her own, and as Henry VIII is recognised as the English card King, so in the quaint lady depicting the Queen we are supposed to see his mother, Elizabeth of York, the wife of King Henry VII. This lady was first betrothed to the Dauphin Charles, the eldest son of Louis XI of France, but this was broken off and in 1486 she married

Henry. By this marriage the Houses of York and Lancaster became united and the terrible Wars of the Roses* were brought to an end. This may have been the reason for the selection of Elizabeth as the Queen to reign over card land, and for over 450 years she has been portrayed in her quaint dress. She is always shown holding the White Rose of York in her hand, a memento that by her marriage the Wars of the Roses came to an end, and to-day, in spite of various usurpers, she seems as firmly fixed on her throne as ever.

The names seen on the French Court cards vary in accordance with the events at the time they were produced. Among others we find Judie, Rachael or Rachel, Argine, Pallas or Palas, Helene, Bersabec, Elisabeth and Dido.

The Queens on an Austrian pack are named RICHELDE, MARGUERITE D'AUTRICHE, JEANNE DE CONSTANTINOPLE and MARIE DE BOURGOGNE.

Singer says that Pallas† on the Queen of Spades was intended to represent Joan of Arc, the Maid of Orleans. Pallas was the goddess of war and of chastity and that is perhaps why Charles VII out of gratitude for the services the Maid had rendered, caused her to be placed under cover of the goddess' name on the cards.

The Knave.

Like the King and Queen, the Knave of the English pack has remained almost unchanged for over 450 years. The costume is evidently copied from the dress of the 15th century and greatly resembles that described by Chaucer in the "Canterbury Tales."

In the old single-ended Court cards the Knave is shown with square cut cap fitting closely to his head wearing a large coat (or gaberdine) with its many coloured ornaments, baggy sleeves and bands, and standing with his parti-coloured, odd-looking, misshapen legs spread wide apart. Figs. 200, 299, 302.

The Knaves of Spades and Hearts are in profile, while the Knave of Diamonds looks to the right and the Knave of Hearts to the left. In a pack in the British Museum, dated 1440, they are shown in exactly similar positions.

* A.D. 1455 to 1486. † Singer, page 118.

Fig. 302 is one of four Knaves, part of an old pack in the British Museum, They were discovered in the covers of an old book in 1841, by Mr. Chatto, who says they date from about 1480. The names on these four knaves are :—

SPADES.	*Hozier.*	DIAMONDS.	*Rolent.*
CLUBS.	*Lancelot.* Fig. 302.	HEARTS.	*Valery.*

The outlines are printed from engraved wood blocks, and the colours probably put on with stencils. Three of these Valets, Rolant, Hozier and Lancelot—are accompanied by dogs.

The book in which these cards were found was a small quarto and formerly belonged to the Cathedral Library of Peterborough, and its subject is the "Sermons of St. Vincent de Ferrer," a Spanish friar who died in 1419.

The name "Jack" often attributed to the English Knave is from the cant name for jester, whilst the expression "Jack-a-Napes" is probably taken from "Jack-a-Naipes," or "Jack of the Cards," the word "Naipes" being the Spanish name for a pack of cards, although Mr. Chatto says it simply means "Jack the Knave."

As shown on the Kings and Queens, the French Court cards have nearly always had names upon them, and on the Knaves, or Valets as they are known in France, we find the names of Hogier, Roland, Lancelot, La Hire, Hector, Annibal, Decius, Horace and Scaevola. A 17th century pack has its Valets named VALETE ECOORT, VARLET DECHASSE, VALET DE HEDI, VALET DE NOBLESSE.

In the old German packs the court cards consist of a King, an Ober or Superior Officer, and an Unter or Under Officer, the latter corresponding to the Knave. Figs. 4 and 90.

On an Austrian pack the Knaves of the four suits are all dressed as Court Jesters.

A Portuguese pack in the Author's collection, shows full length figures on all the Coat cards and each of the four Knaves holds a large long-handled axe. The Knave of Clubs is also holding a shield bearing the arms of Portugal and the word Lisbon upon it.

During the French Revolution the Kings, Queens and Knaves were denominated respectively Genie (Genius), Liberte (Liberty), and Egalite (Equality). On one pack the Court cards are as follows:

	Hearts.	*Clubs.*	*Diamonds.*	*Spades.*
KINGS	GENIE DES ARTS.	GENIE DE LA PAIX.	GENIE DE COMMERCE.	GENIE DE LA GUERRE.
QUEENS.	LIBERTE DE LA PRESSE.	LIBERTE DU MARIAGE.	LIBERTE DES PROFESSIONS.	LIBERTE DES CULTES.
KNAVES.	EGALITE DE DEVOIRS.	EGALITE DE COULEURS.	EGALITE DE BANCS.	EGALITE DE DROITS.

The four Queens are holding staves each surmounted by the Cap of Liberty, and both Kings and Knaves are rather rough-looking creatures whether as men of "Genius" or of "Liberty."

The Ace.

Generally the value of the cards are KING, QUEEN, KNAVE, ten, nine, and so on down to the ACE, which is the lowest, and yet there seems to be no uniformity as to the value of the Ace. In some games (as in Whist) it is the highest for value, but in cutting it remains the lowest, and in some other games it comes after the fives. In Piquet it is the highest both for cutting and playing, but in Ecarte the value of the Ace comes between the Knave and the Ten.

The explanation why the lowest number (the Ace) became of the highest value is, perhaps, that many changes took place at various times as to the number of cards in each pack, and, supposing the Tarocchi pack of seventy-eight to have been the first used, we find that the Florentines increased the pack to ninety-seven, but a little later the Bolognese reduced it to forty numerals with the addition of the twenty-two Atouts, rejecting the two, three, four and five of each suit, making a pack of sixty-two. These were used in the game called Tarocchino. Later still the pack was reduced to forty, and the game played was Trappola. Eventually the pack became as we now know it, forty numerals and twelve Coat cards (the four Chevaliers of each suit being left out) thus reducing the pack from fifty-six to fifty-two, and the Ace was probably raised to the highest place in the pack on the loss of one of the Coat Cards in order to preserve the original number of superior value.

On page 207 there will be found the names by which the Ace is known in the various European countries.

North American Indian.

The Apache Indian tribes of North America seem to have taken as their model the suits and signs used by the Spaniards, such as the Cup, Sword, Money and Stick or Baton. They paint these on small pieces of deerskin in red and blue, and generally they are very roughly drawn and coloured, but the signs are easily distinguished.

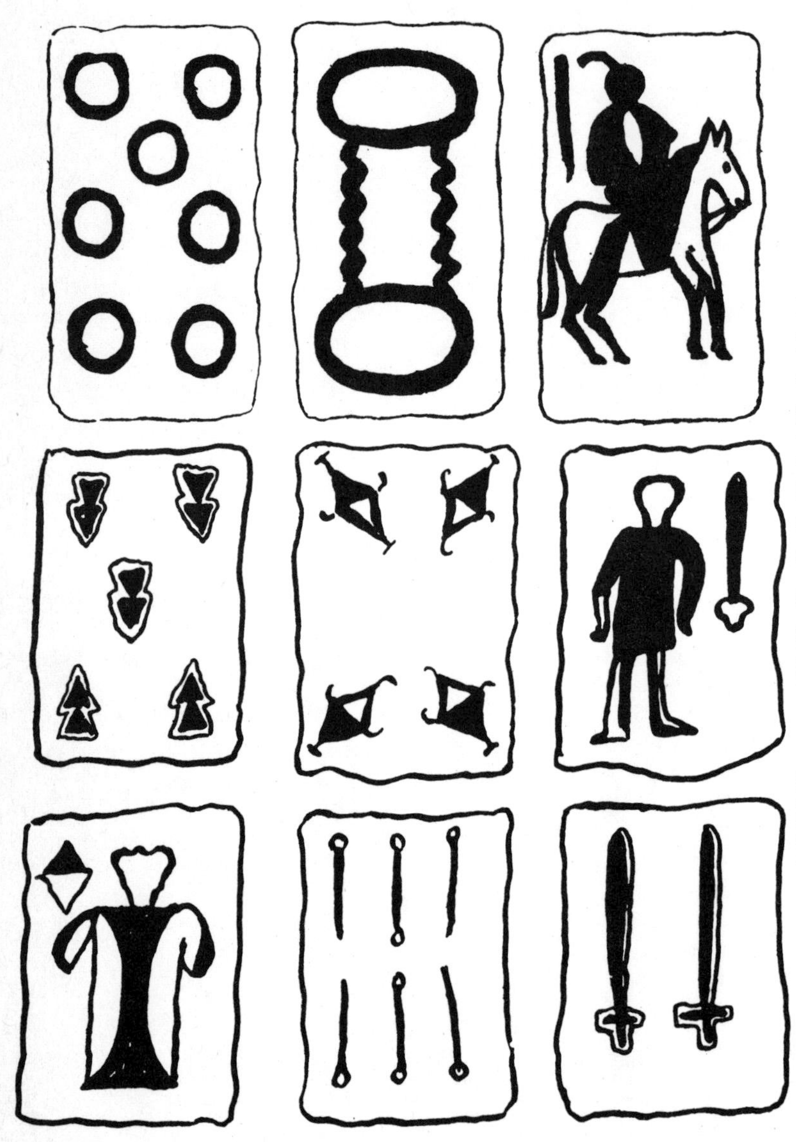

The nine cards illustrated probably represent the seven and two of money, the Chevalier of Batons, the five and four of Cups, Valet of Swords, King of Cups, six of Batons and two of Swords, as used on the Spanish cards.

There is one of these deerskin packs in the Museum at Boston.

Fig. 303.

Names of Cards.

Dr. Beuchan says of the packs of 52 cards that "The 12 Honours of the pack are emblematic of the 12 signs of the Zodiac, also the 12 months of the Solar Year, and each of these is divided into thirty degrees, as the honour cards are equivalent to ten in value, and if we multiply 30 by 12 = 360, we have the number of days in the ancient Egyptian year, and equal to the number of degrees into which the equator is still divided. The colours Red and Black answer to the great division of the year into two equal parts, from solstice to solstice and equinox to equinox. The four suits indicate the four seasons. The whole number of cards in the pack is 52, equal to the number of weeks in the year, and the number of cards in each suit is thirteen, the same number as the weeks in each quarter of the year."

The various names by which Playing Cards are known in the European countries are as follows :—

France – –	Cartes a jouer.
Germany – –	Karten *or* Spielkarten.
Holland – –	Kaarten.
Russia – –	Kartii.
Italy – – –	Naibi.
Spain – – –	Naypes.
Portugal – –	Naipe.
Denmark – –	Kort or Spielkort.

The equivalent names used in European countries for the four suits and the aces are :—

Tarot Cards	England.	France.	Italy.	Spain.	Germany.	Holland.
Money.	Diamonds.	Carreaux.	Danari.	Oros.	Rauten.	Ruyten.
Batons.	Clubs.	Trefles.	Bastoni.	Bastos.	Kreuzen.	Klaver.
Swords.	Spades.	Piques.	Spade.	Espadas.	Spaten.	Scop.
Cups	Hearts.	Cœurs.	Coppe.	Copas.	Herzen.	Harten.
Asso.	Ace.	As.	Asso.	As.	Asz.	Aas.

Names of the Coat or Court Cards.

Italy	Re.	Regina.	Cavallo.	Faute
Spain..........	Rey.	Reyna.	Caballo.	Stoa.
Germany	Konig.	Ober-mann.		Unter-mann.
France.........	Roi.	Dame.		Valet.
England	King.	Queen.		Knave or Jack.

Suit Signs.

While nearly all European countries to-day are using the four suits, DIAMONDS, SPADES, CLUBS AND HEARTS there are many other signs which are or have been in use among various nations. In Spain, Italy, and Portugal we have CUPS, SWORDS, MONEY AND WANDS. In Germany LEAVES, ACORNS, HEARTS AND BELLS. On the English pack described on page 161 we have ACORNS, DIAMONDS, HEARTS AND SWORDS, and on another English pack page 159 the suits are DIAMONDS, SHAMROCK LEAVES, CUPS AND SWORDS. On the French Heraldic pack (date *circa* 1672) are FLEUR-DE-LYS (for France), LIONS (for Spain), EAGLES (for Germany), and ROSES (for Italy) page 105.

The interesting pack engraved by Jost Ammon, page 79, has for the four suits PRINTERS' INKING BALLS, WINE VASES, METAL DRINKING CUPS and BOOKS. The circular cards, page 111, bear the suits PARROTS, HARES, COLUMBINES and PINKS.

Thomas Murner, the Minorite Friar of the order of St. Francis, who is said to have been the first to attempt to use playing cards for the purpose of instruction, used various suit signs, according to the subject he wished to teach, and we find Bells, Fish, Acorns, Suns, Stars, Pigeons, Crabs, Crescents, Crowns, Cats, Shields, Turbans, Swallows, Hearts, Scorpions and Wreaths of Serpents. He was a teacher of philosophy at Friburg early in the XVI century. Page 76.

A variation of one of the signs is seen on the cards on page 70, where pomegranates are used either instead of the sign of Money on the Italian cards or instead of the Bells of the German pack.

The suits of the cards used in China, India and Japan are again quite different from any of the above.

The Hindustan pack of Ivory cards, page 52, consists of seven suits, viz. :—SUNS, MOONS, CROWNS, CUSHIONS, HARPS, LETTERS and SWORDS. Again on another Hindustan pack, page 56, the ten suits are the emblems of the Ten Avators of Vishnou.

A French pack of the middle of the XVII century has the four suits of DIAMONDS, CLUBS, HEARTS and SPADES, but only one pip on each card, the value being shown by various numbers of Birds, Flowers, Fruit and Animals. For instance, the four of diamonds is indicated by one red diamond and four large apples; the two of clubs by a single club and two baskets of fruit, and so on.

These are some of the numerous suit signs which have been or are being used on the cards and the selections given will help the reader to form some idea of their great variety.

Taxes on Playing Cards.

A tax was levied upon playing cards as early as the reign of James I, as is shown in a minute of some state papers dated July 20th, 1615, at Westminster.

"Letters patent granting Sir Richard Coningsby, for a rent of £200 per annum, the imposition of 5*s*. per gross on playing cards and the office of Inspector of all playing cards imported, in recompense of £1800 due to him from the King, and of his patent for the export of Tin, granted by the late Queen."

A letter from the Lord Treasurer confirms this grant "to Sir Richard Coningsby, Knight, under the Greate Seale of England."

In the reign of Queen Anne it was proposed that a duty of sixpence should be paid on each pack of cards for a term of thirty-two years, commencing June 11th, 1711, in order to obtain funds "for carrying on the war, and for other her Majesty's Occasions."

Many protests and petitions came from the importers of paper as well as from the makers of playing cards, and one which was presented to Parliament finishes thus:—

"Wherefore it is humbly hoped that your Honours will not lay a Duty which it's humbly conceived will bring no profit to the QUEEN, *but inevitably ruin many hundreds of her subjects."*

But, appealing as this petition was, *Her Majesty's "Occasions"* were in such a bad way that it failed to move Parliament, and the Act became law. It was made felony, punishable by death, to counterfeit or forge the Seal, or the marks which denoted that the duty had been paid. At a later date an engraver named Harding was actually executed for engraving a duty ace of spades which had been ordered by a card maker, who, to save his own life, escaped from the country.

A broadside, dated 1643, gives particulars of a proclamation:—

> "Order by Committee appointed by parliament for the Navy and Customs, on the complaint by the Cardmakers of London, likely to perish by reason of divers merchants bringing in Playing Cards into this Kingdom."

Also a proclamation from Whitehall, dated 1684, as follows:—

> "A proclamation prohibiting the importing of Foreign Playing Cards, and for seizing such as are or shall be imported."

The following is a copy of a petition which is in the Books Department of the British Museum.

QUEEN ANNE, CIR. 1710. LONDON.*

"Reasons Humbly offer'd by the Card-makers against the Tax upon Playing-Cards."

"The Card-makers in and about the City of London are about One Hundred Master Workmen. For some time past (Paper having been double the Price as formerly) the trade is much Decayed.

"The most they sell their Cards for to the Retailers (one sort with another) is Three Half-pence the Pack, and their Profit not above an Half-penny. So that the Tax intended will be double the value of the Cards and six times their gain.

"The generality of the Card-makers are Poor men and out of the Small Gains above can hardly maintain their families: And therefore to impose a Tax to be immediately paid upon making by the Cardmakers (whose Stocks and Abilities are so very mean, that they now make hard shift to forbear the Retailers the Ordinary time of Credit) will be a direct way to Ruine these Poor Men.

"Besides there is at present a Stock of Cards in the retailers hands sufficient for the consumption of Four or Five year; and they will assuredly sell all the old stock off before they take any at the New advanced rate: The consequence whereof will be:

"*First.* That the Cardmakers till that stock be sold off can make no new ones.

"*Secondly.* That during that time they and their Families must needs starve.

"*Lastly.* That until the card-makers can make new ones no money can arise by such Tax."

One of the petitions reads:—

"Her Majesty's customs arising from the importation of Geneo paper will be extremely lessen'd: f'it is reasonably supposed that there are 40,000 Rheams of Geneo paper annually used in this (playing cards) manufacture."

*Willshire, page 313.

Old Method of Manufacture.

Fig. 304, made from an old opaque water colour of date about 1690, shows the workshop of a maker of playing cards, and the various processes of printing, stencilling, drying, examining, packing and even selling, can be plainly seen.

Fig. 304.

In 1441 the master card makers of Venice obtained from their Senate an order forbidding the introduction of printed and painted cards from outside the city. And as printed cards are especially mentioned it would appear that some process other than printing with the stencil was known, and it is probable that the first printing executed from blocks of wood was for the making of playing cards, and as by the year 1460 the use of cards had spread into nearly every country in Europe, the necessity for a cheap and rapid method of producing them in large quantities would arise.

An old chronicler of the city of Ulm, of about the year 1397 states "that playing cards have been sent in bundles to Italy, Sicily and other southern countries in exchange for groceries and other Merchandice." and it is possible that this exportation of "bundles" of playing cards from Germany was the reason why the edict forbidding the importation of cards into Venice in 1441 was made.* It also points to their having been manufactured in quantities even before 1423, the date of the earliest known wood-cut.†

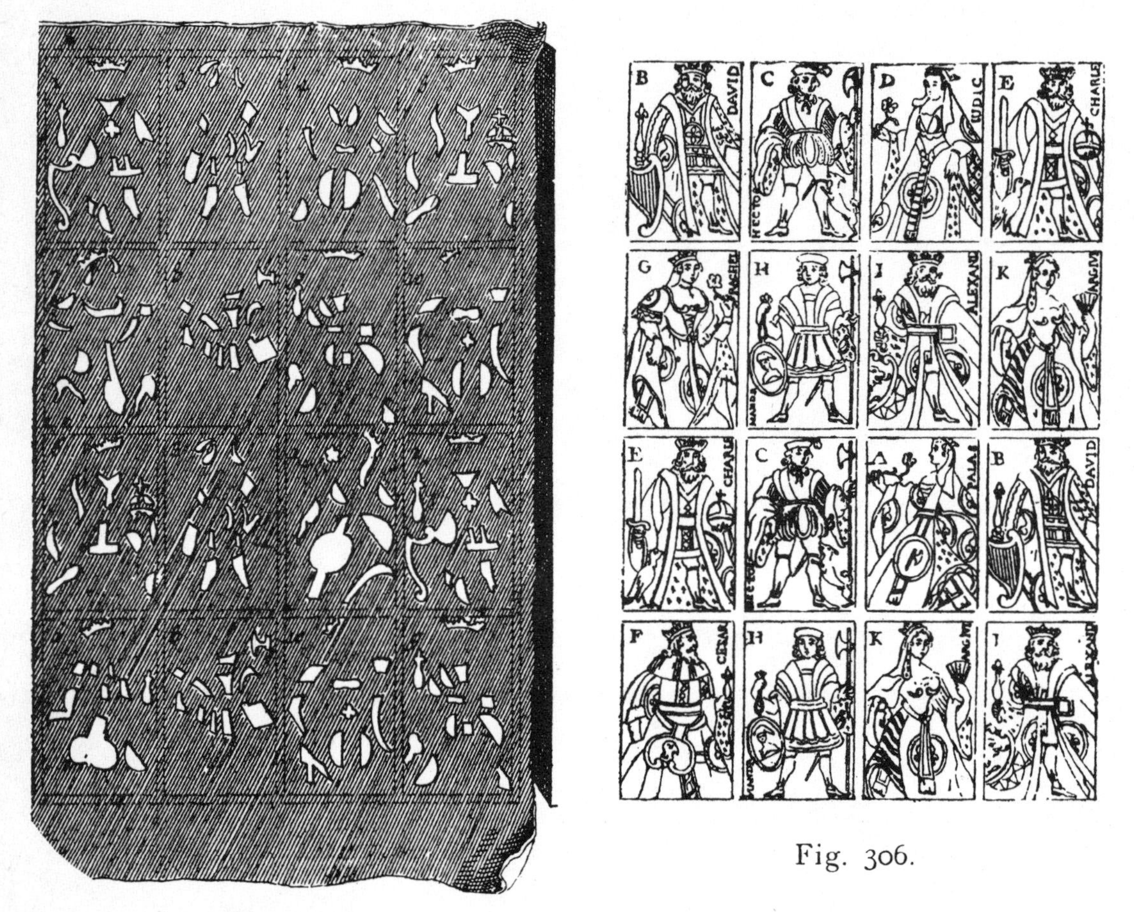

Fig. 305.

Fig. 306.

The illustration, Fig. 305, shows the method of colouring the cards by means of a stencil. On the right is shown the print in outline ready for colouring, and it can easily be seen how when the stencil shown on the left is placed over the print, certain parts will be coloured, and for each different colour required another stencil would be used to cover the other parts of the print in the same way.

* Devils Picture Books, page 37. † Said to have been known in China in the 6th century.

In a little volume called "The Book of Trades" there are various woodcuts from the designs of Jost Ammon,* and one of these shows a painter of cards at work, and gives direct proof of the means used to colour cards, and woodcuts: the artist is using a stencil and large flat brush, and several pots of colour and more brushes are on a bench at his side. Breitkopf, writing in 1784, gives the following account of the process† "Their method of enlivening their woodcuts with colour was extremely simple. It was not done singly, figure by figure, and stroke by stroke

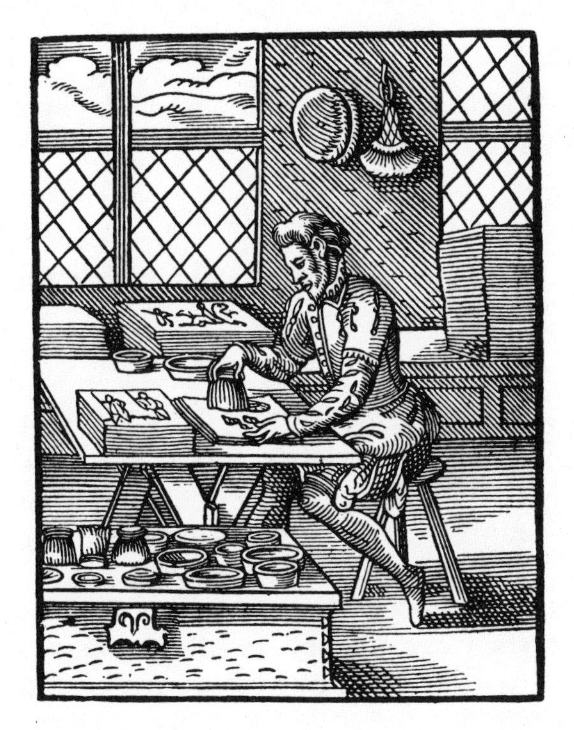

Fig. 307.

with small pencils: but the whole sheet was covered at once with colour by means of large flat brushes. They took pasteboard, pasted the impression of their print upon it, and cut out all the parts of it which were to receive the same colours. Thus they formed as many pierced pieces of pasteboard, called *Patronen* (stencils) as there were colours in the painting or design." Fig. 307.

* Pages 78 to 82.

† Breitkopf und Roch Ursprung der Holzschneidekunst, page 161.

‡ Singer, page 179.

Copy of letter from

"THE LADY'S MAGAZINE," 1808.

To the Editor of the Lady's Magazine.

Sir,

By giving insertion to the following humble apology for the polite amusement of card-playing you will much oblige.

Your constant Reader,

and occasional Correspondent,

E.H.

"Among the all various subjects of satire and ridicule that have from time to time employed the reformers, or rather pretended reformers, of the times, cards have long been the established butt of malevolence and ill-nature. All ranks and degrees of writers, from the grave sermonising declaimer, to the facetious fabricator of the pointed epigram, have constantly been profuse in pouring out their invectives against this prevailing malady, as they are pleased to denominate it. Strange, that among all the vices and follies that infest the age this poor amusement should still be pointed out as one of the grand objects of ridicule and rise superior to all the united efforts of its enemies, equally unshaken by the elaborate dissertations of serious moralisers; and all the shafts of satire and ridicule aimed at it by professed wits. It is an amusement equally adapted to all ranks and conditions. The cobler has a mind as capable of enjoying it as the courtier; nor can it communicate a more elevated or refined pleasure to the duchess who figures on the very meridian of the *ton* than it does to her whose *eclat* extends no further than the delicate abodes of Billingsgate. Shall then such a noble invention, with all its attendant pleasures, and unnumbered advantages, fall a sacrifice to the attacks of a few ill-natured scribblers."

Ombre—Pepy's Diary.

This game of Ombre seems to have been one of the favourite games among Royalty, and it is said to have been introduced into England by Catherine of Portugal. It was played at a triangular or three-sided table with 40 cards, the 8, 9 and 10 of each suit being discarded.

GAME OF OMBRE. Fig. 308.
From a print in "Seymour's Compleat Gamester" 1734.

Pepys, writing in his Diary of February 17th, 1667, says :—

"This evening, going to the Queene's side, to see the ladies, I did finde the Queen, the Duchesse of York, and another or two, at cards with the room full of ladies and great men, which I was amazed at to see on a Sunday, having not believed it, but, contrarily, flatly denied the same a little while since to my cousin Roger Pepys."

Alexander Pope's Description.

Pope, in his epic poem, "The Rape of the Lock," gives us in poetic form a description of the faces of the cards as known in his time:

" Belinda now, whom thirst of Fame invites,
Burns to encounter two advent'rous Knights
At Ombre, singly to decide their doom,
And swells her breast with conquest yet to come. . . . .

Behold, four Kings in majesty rever'd
With hoary whiskers, and a forky beard:
And four fair Queens, whose hands sustain a flower,
Th' expressive emblem of their softer power;
Four Knaves in garb succinct, a trusty band,
Caps on their heads, and halberds in their hand
And party-colour'd troops, a shining train,
Drawn forth to combat on the velvet plain,
The skilful nymph reviews her force with care;
Let Spades be trumps, she said; and trumps they were. . . . .

The Baron now his Diamonds pours apace;
Th' embroider'd king who shows but half his face,
And his refulgent queen, with powers combin'd,
Of broken troops an easy conquest find.
Club, Diamonds, Hearts, in wild disorder seen,
With throngs promiscuous strew the level green.

The Knave of Diamonds tries his wily arts,
And wins (O shameful chance!) the Queen of Hearts.
At this the blood the virgin's cheeks forsook,
A livid paleness spreads o'er all her look;
She sees and trembles at th' approaching ill,
Just in the jaws of ruin, and Codille.
And now (as oft in some distemper'd state)
On one nice trick depends the gen'ral fate;
An Ace of Hearts steps forth: the King unseen
Lurk'd in her hand, and mourn'd his captive Queen;
He springs to vengeance with an eager pace,
And falls like thunder on the prostrate Ace.
The Nymph exulting, fills with shouts the sky;
The walls, the woods, and long canals reply."

The Soldier's Almanack.

A book on Playing Cards would not be complete without the old story of the "SOLDIER'S ALMANACK, BIBLE AND PRAYER BOOK," which was a favourite with our forefathers, at the beginning of the 19th century. There have been various versions published, one in Brussels as far back as 1778, another in Paris 1809, but the basis of the story is practically the same in each case, and the following abbreviated version gives a good idea of them all.

"RICHARD MIDDLETON, a soldier, attending divine service, with the rest of the regiment at a church, instead of pulling out a Bible to find the parson's text, spread a pack of cards before him. This singular behaviour did not long pass unnoticed, both by the clergyman and the serjeant of the company; the latter in particular requested him to put up the cards, and on his refusal, conducted him after church before the Mayor, to whom he preferred a formal complaint of Richard's indecent behaviour during divine service. 'Well, soldier!' (said the Mayor) 'what excuse have you for this strange scandalous behaviour? If you can make any apology, it's well; if you cannot, I will cause you to be severely punished for it.' 'Since your honour is so good,' replied Richard, 'I will inform you. On saying this, Richard drew out his pack of cards, and presenting one of the aces to the Mayor, continued his address to the magistrate as follows:

"'When I see an Ace, it reminds me that there is only one God; and when I look upon a Two or a Three, the former puts me in mind of the Father and Son, and the latter of the Father, Son, and Holy Ghost. A Four calls for remembrance the Four Evangelists, Matthew, Mark, Luke, and John, A Five, the five wise Virgins who were ordered to trim their lamps. A Six, that in Six days God created heaven and earth. A Seven, that on the seventh day he rested. An Eight, of the eight righteous persons preserved from the deluge. A Nine, of the nine lepers cleansed by our Saviour. And a Ten, of the ten commandments that God gave Moses on Mount Sinai, on the two tables of stone.' He took the Knave and put it aside. 'When I see the Queen, it puts me in mind of the Queen of Sheba. And when I see the King, it puts me in mind of the Great King of Heaven and Earth, which is God Almighty; and likewise his Majesty King George the Fourth.' 'Well,' said the Mayor, 'you have given a good description of all the cards except one, which is lacking.' 'Which is that?' said the soldier. 'The Knave,' said the Mayor.

"'If your honour will not be angry with me,' returned Richard, 'I can give you the same satisfaction on that as any in the pack?'. 'The greatest knave that I know is the serjeant who brought me before you.' 'I don't know,' replied the Mayor, 'whether he be the greatest knave or no; but I am sure he is the greatest fool.'

"The soldier then continued as follows: 'When I count how many cards are in a pack, I find there are 52,—so many weeks are there in a year. When I reckon how many tricks are won by a pack, I find there are 13,—so many months are there in a year. So that this pack of cards is both Bible, Almanack, and Prayer Book to me.'

"The Mayor called his servants, ordered them to entertain the soldier well, gave him a piece of money, and said he was the cleverest fellow he had ever heard in his life."

A NEW

Game at Cards,

BETWEEN

A Nobleman in London,

AND

One of his Servants,

FIRST SHEWING.

How the Servant converts his Cards into a complete Almanack, by which he divides the Year into Months, Weeks, Days, Hours, and Minutes. He likewiſe forms them into a Monitor, or a Prayer Book.—The whole being an Entertainment to the Curious and Ingenious, as well as the Learned and Serious. The like was never before Publiſhed.

J. Pitts, Printer, and Wholesale Toy Warehouse 6, Great st andrew Street 7 Dials.

Fig. 309.

Here is another version published by "*J. Pitts, Printer, 6 Greta st. Andrew's Street, 7 Dials.*" in the form of a small chap-book entitled "A new Game at Cards," the front page of which is reproduced in Fig. 309 and one inside page in Fig. 310. This varies somewhat, as it is supposed to be a conversation between a nobleman and his servant, who being denounced as a gambler, denies the charge, and proceeds to clear himself in much the same way as the Soldier in the other version. We are told by the printer that "*The Like was never before Published.*" A very badly executed wood-cut shows the servant (?) exhibiting the five of Diamonds and on the table we can see the two of Clubs. The end of the story tells us that "Jack was forgiven and the one who informed against him was told to take his wages and walk."

The King puts me in mind of the allegiance I owe to his Majeſty.

The Queen puts me in mind of the allegiance I owe to her Majeſty

When I come to the Ten, it puts me in mind of the Ten Commandments, Likewiſe reminds me of the Ten Tribes of Israel that were cut off, in their wickedneſs.

The Nine, puts me in mind of the Nine Muses, and alſo the nine noble orders practiſed by Men,

When I come to the Eight, it puts me in mind of the Eight Altitudes, and alſo the Eight Perſons that were ſaved in Noah's Ark.

The Seven puts me in mind of the Seven Wonders of the World, and alſo the Seven Planets, that rule the Days of the Week.

Fig. 310.

ARDHANARI.

Holding the Wand, Cup, Sword and Ring.

It is interesting to note that the four suit signs, Money, Cups, Swords and Batons, which are found on the old Italian and Spanish cards, are also shown in a picture of the ancient Hindostanee Deity known as ARDHANARI. This is a composite god, the left half being SHIVA* and the right half DEVI (DURGA). SHIVA holds in his hands the Cup and the Wand, and behind him is his vehicle, the Bull. DEVI is holding the Sword and the Ring, and her vehicle the Tiger, is crouching behind her.

Fig. 311.

As already suggested it is surely more than a coincidence that all these four signs—not one or two; but all four—should be the same as the four which were used on the oldest known European cards when they were first introduced from the East.**

Hanuman, one of the inferior dieties, who was the son of Vaya, the god of the winds, holds in four of his hands, a Cup, a Sword, a Ring and a Sceptre.‡

The same four signs are still used on the Spanish playing cards and are generally recognised as being the symbols of the four chief castes into which men are divided on the banks of the Ganges and the Nile. The Cup denotes the Priesthood, the Sword implies the King or a Soldier, the Circle or Ring in the hands of the merchant becomes Money, and the Staff or Baton is emblematic of the tiller of the soil.

** Page 21. * ‡ Page 64.

A humorous engraving by George Cruikshank is shown in Fig. 312. The Knave of Hearts is seated, as Chairman, on a stage, and the Knave of Spades is addressing a pack of Knave Cards which are cleverly drawn to represent an audience. The speaker commences:—

> "*Knaves, Shufflers, Blacklegs and Brothers, the game is getting desperate, a pack of fellows want to spoil our sport, shut up our betting shops and destroy our counters.* (CRIES OF "SHAME.")
>
> "*Yes, want us to cut our Clubs, break our Hearts and put us under the Turf with our own Spades, but we'll see if Diamond can't cut Diamond.*" (HEAR, HEAR, AND LOUD APPLAUSE).
>
> "*Yes, not only that, but wants us to be sober as well as Honest* (OH, OH, OH, WITH SHOUTS OF LAUGHTER).—"*Why, we must go to Parliament, there are lots of Trump-cards in the 'Lords and Commons,' the Nobs of Aristocracy.'* "

The above are extracts from the speech. At the bottom is the title—

> "*A pack of Knaves, or a 'Packed' Meeting of the Knowing Cards of the betting shop interest to consider and adopt the best Shuffling Tricks to carry on their Game.*"—*a humble attempt in the pre-Raphaelite style by George Cruikshank.*

Fig. 312.

Stories of Gamblers and Gambling.

There is a story of a king who, having a great aversion to gambling of all kinds, prohibited it throughout his kingdom, and tried to do away with everything which in anyway aided the vice, such as cards, dice, &c. Anyone found using such things was threatened with severe penalties. However his spies soon discovered that a number of the king's subjects were meeting at a certain place and that large sums of money were said to be lost and won. A spy was sent to investigate, but he could discover nothing which could be deemed gambling, as no cards or dice appeared to be in use. Yet now and again certain faces would light up with strange, unaccountable looks of joy, while others wore an equally unaccountable expression of gloom, and money was continually passing from one person to another. The spy returned to his sovereign to report his failure, and it was not until a long time afterwards that the King learned how his nobles had ignored his commands without being found out. They had simply arranged among themselves to keep their eyes on certain panes of glass in the room where they were quietly sitting, each one having selected a particular pane as his own, and the one on whose pane the greatest number of flies alighted in a given time was accounted the winner.

The story shows that gaming does not depend alone upon cards, although for centuries they have been condemned as the chief cause of gambling. Where the passion for play exists the absence of cards will not extinguish the gambling spirit, and other means to satisfy the craving will soon be discovered.

About 1716, Law, the great speculator, came to Paris, and in partnership with a famous tragedy queen, set up a gambling house, and was soon one of the wealthiest persons in the land. His personality was pleasing, and he was much in request among the fashionable society of Paris. He is said to have won, in a very short time, sixty-seven thousand pounds. Play for high stakes was the order of the day, and the Duchess of Berri lost in one night the sum of one million seven hundred livres.*

Paris became a nest of gambling-houses, and play went on from morning until night and from night until morning, without intermission. Everyone, from the highest to the lowest, became infected with the gambling spirit, and as the result, "everything became vulgarised,

* St. Simon, Vol. XVIII, page 162.

royalty was growing coarse, the nobility gross, and the magistracy venal. The growing evil was beyond arrest; and though a justiciary ordinance was published in 1760, fixing the limit of losses at one hundred pistoles, it was generally disregarded. Charles II, in England, had already determined the limit at one hundred pounds; but high play and great losses continued the custom."*

The hope of winning great fortunes has always appealed to the adventurer, who will use any means to gain his end. A certain Calzado, with another "Greek" named Garcia, were summoned before the court, and charged with cheating and using "doctored" cards. Garcia, who had left France, was condemned in his absence to five years imprisonment and Calzado to fifteen months, and both were fined very severely. It was told of Calzado that he once went to Havannah and bought up every pack of cards in the place, and then quietly awaited the arrival of a vessel by which he had arranged for a consignment of marked cards to be landed. His winnings were considerable, but his manœuvre was discovered, and he had to leave rather hurriedly.

There was a famous card-sharper of the time of King Charles named Clancy. He was a major in the King's army and at one time resided in St. Martin's Lane. As might be expected, he got into financial difficulties, and looking one day from his window, saw a bailiff's man waiting for him to appear. In order to rest, this gentleman had seated himself on the edge of a joiner's stall just opposite Clancy's lodgings. Clancy sent his servant to bid the joiner's apprentice come to him, and the lad was promised a crown if he could manage to nail the bailiff's man by his leathern belt to the stall. This he managed to do. Presently a coach rattled up to Clancy's door, and he rushed out and got into it. The bailiff's man jumped up to arrest him, and as he did so the whole structure upon which he had been resting came down with a mighty clatter, amidst which the card-sharper disappeared. In 1660, at the age of 39, Clancy was hanged at Tyburn.

Another gambler and cheat, Sir John Johnson, is said to have used the slip at put and pegged forward at cribbage. He was hanged on the 23rd December, 1690, at the age of 42.

* page 24.

Spain has been credited with the invention of several games, and claims that *Primero* was first played in that country, although the national game was and is *Ombre*, a most complicated game played with forty cards only, the eights, nines and tens being discarded.

Rosny, Duc de Sully, the friend of Henry IV of France, while he always refrained from play himself, had continually to pay the debts of his royal master, who was a great gambler and played for very high stakes.*

In his *Economics Royales* Sully accuses Henry of an inordinate love of gaming, and states that by his example he was indirectly the ruin of many wealthy families, and gives particulars of several considerable sums squandered in play by Henry. A letter from the King dated 1609 reads

> My friend—" I have lost at play twenty-two thousand pistoles† I pray you to remit them incontinently by the hands of the bearer, Feideau, that so he may distribute them among the persons to whom I am indebted, according to my order."
>
> Adieu, my friend,
>
> Henry.

Of course, the necessary funds to pay these debts had to be raised at once to save the king's honour, who would call upon his minister a few days later to beg his pardon and promise to be less extravagant in future. Sully adds, that he had taken note of several considerable sums squandered in play by Henry, but these were by no means all; In 1607, Henry writes that certain merchants held him for a sum of 9000 livres, which he had dissipated at the fair of St. Germains. He was still worse later, for there is an entry for 22000 pistoles (about £18,000) lost at play, of which about 700,000 francs were due to the Portuguese Edward Fernandes,

Following the example of the king and his court, the practice spread among the citizens; gaming houses were set up and let for enormous sums and it was not until 1610, when the king was assassinated by Ravaillac‡ that an attempt was made to put a stop to the gambling spirit which had seized the whole nation.

* Memoires de Sully, page 176. † about 17/-.

‡ "The death of Ravaillac is one of the most dreadful on record. He was first burned at a slow fire. Then his flesh torn with red hot pincers, and melted lead and oil poured into gaping wounds, and when four horses fastened to him, failed to pull his limbs to pieces, the executioner cut him into four quarters."

Cardinal Mazarin, a great dignitary of the Church of Rome and Prime Minister of Louis XIV, was much given to cheating at cards. His rage for card playing was such that he almost died with the cards in his hand. Paul de la Roche painted a picture of the Cardinal upon his death-bed. He is there represented as being unable to play himself, but is employing others to play for him. His eyes sparkle, and he watches the game as eagerly as if he were playing himself. The picture illustrates no fictitious incident. Contemporaries testify to its fidelity.

The Duchess of Mazarin, a niece of the Cardinal, who resided in England, is said to have lost a fortune of twenty-five millions of livres, left her by her uncle the Cardinal. She died insolvent as well as insane.

In the reign of Queen Anne card playing seems to have attained the full tide of its popularity in every part of civilised Europe. In England it had become both fashionable and popular. The game of Ombre was in favour with the ladies, while the gentlemen preferred Piquet. Clergymen and country squires played Whist, and the labouring classes played All Fours, Cribbage, etc.

Sir Roger de Coverley is said to have sent a string of hogs' puddings and a pack of cards as a Christmas gift to every poor family in the parish.

When the South Sea Bubble stock jobbing scheme burst, its promoters and their dupes were caricatured in a pack of cards brought out about 1721.

Dr. Johnson regretted that he had not learned to play cards, giving as his reason "that it is very useful in life; it generates kindness, and consolidates society."

The Nine of Diamonds is known as the Curse of Scotland. The story runs thus. "When the Duke of Cumberland was waging war against Bonnie Prince Charlie, he indulged in drinking bouts between the battles, and on one such occasion scribbled on the back of a Nine of Diamonds an order for the massacre of the unoffending and unsuspecting inhabitants, the Macdonalds (a Jacobite clan) for not surrendering before January 1st, 1692, the time stated in King William's proclamation. Sir

John Dalrymple, master, (afterward Earl of Stair), obtained a decree 'to extirpate that set of thieves,' and the arms of the Earls of Stair are to-day emblazoned as 'Or ; on a saltier azure nine lozenges of the first.' The nine lozenges or diamonds are reminiscent of the massacre at Glencoe, for which the Earl was blamed.

The Knave of Clubs is connected with a story of the time when Queen Mary determined to stamp out Protestantism in Ireland. She sent a certain Dr. Cole there, with a commission for a general massacre, and on the way while stopping at Chester, he boasted in public of the object of his mission. His landlady, who was a Protestant, overheard him, and before he left she contrived to open the tin box containing the order, extract his own papers and substitute some blank paper with the Knave of clubs on the top. The Doctor only discovered the trick when he reached Ireland, and hurried back for a new order, but the Queen had died in the meantime and Elizabeth was on the throne, and there was no massacre—thanks to the Knave of Clubs.

The Gallant Dupe.

Fig. 313.

Pack issued in 1692.
To Teach Carving.

All the Flesh of Beasts are rang'd among ye Suit of Harts,
All the fowl among the Suit of Dymonds,
All ye bak'd meats among the Suit of Spades,
And all the Fish among the Suit of Clubs.

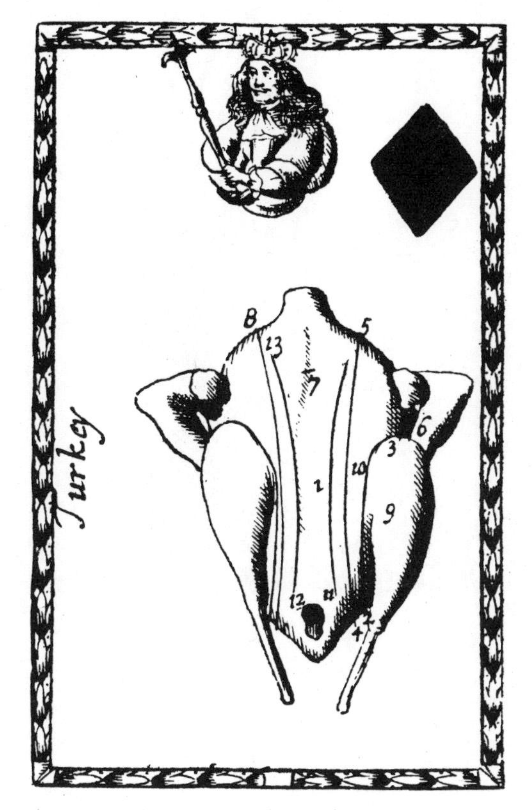

King of Diamonds.

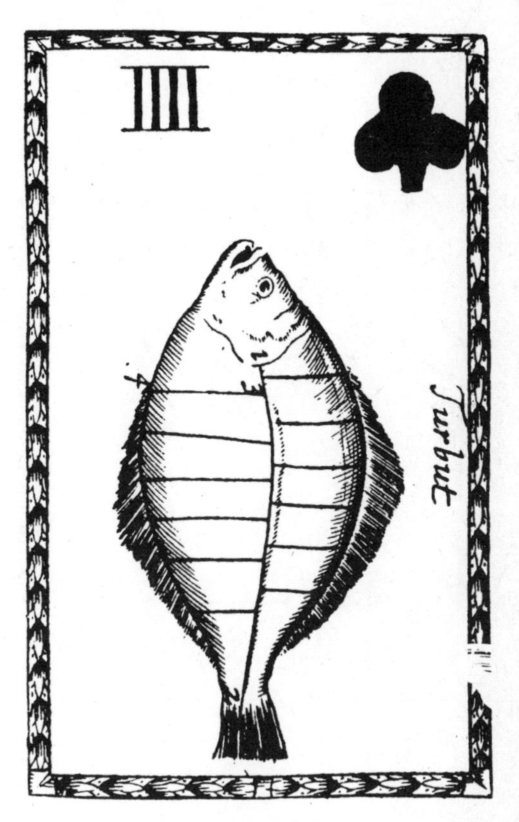

Four of Clubs.

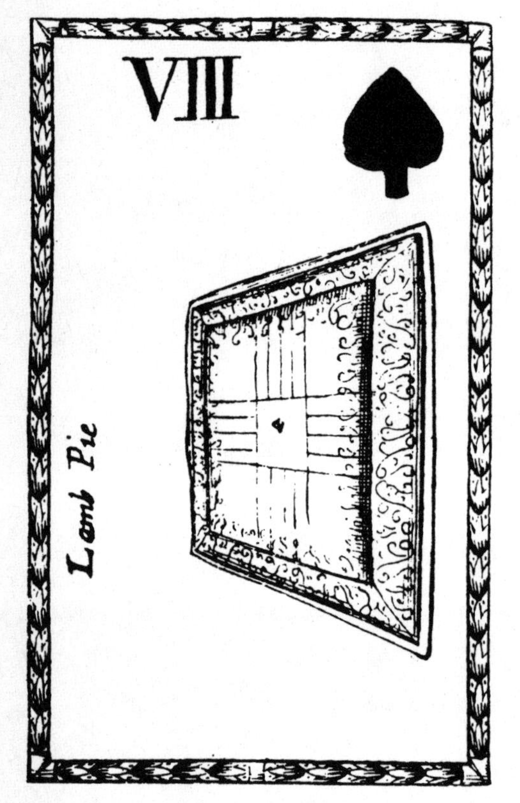

Eight of Spades.

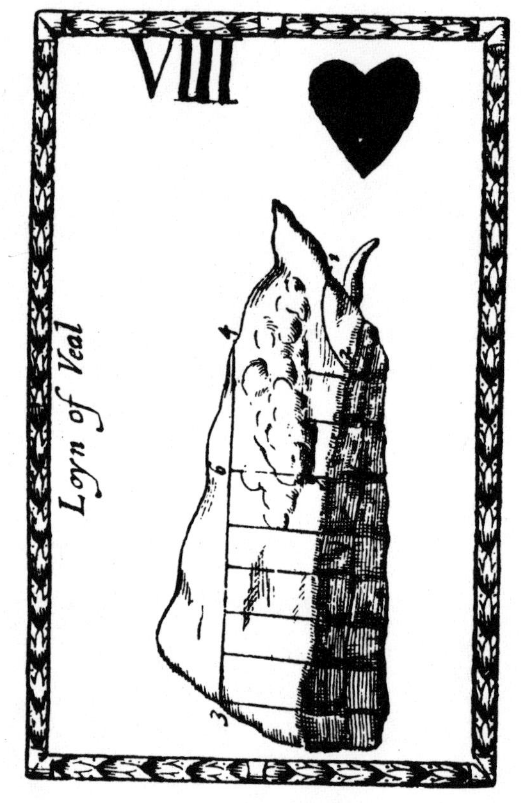

Eight of Hearts.

INDEX